# KINETIC
# FAMILY
# DRAWINGS
# (K-F-D)

# KINETIC FAMILY DRAWINGS (K-F-D)

## An Introduction to Understanding Children through Kinetic Drawings

By Robert C. Burns

*Director, Psychology, Children's Orthopedic Hospital and Medical Center;
Clinical Assistant Professor, Department of Pediatrics, University of Washington
School of Medicine (Seattle); Director, Seattle Institute of Human Development*

and S. Harvard Kaufman, M.D.

*Clinical Professor of Psychiatry, Department of Psychiatry, University
of Washington School of Medicine (Seattle)*

**BRUNNER/MAZEL, Publishers • New York**

# FOREWORD

Why would analytically-oriented authors ask a non-Freudian neuropsychologist to write a foreword to their book? The answer to this question, I believe, lies in the book and the delightful spirit in which it was written. The authors obviously have just the right "light" touch. Translated into scientific jargon, this means the authors are not afraid to generate, use, and possibly reject a large number of hypotheses about children based on their action-drawings. They clearly understand that the emergence of difficulties in the development of a child is a complex, multi-factorial process, and that their efforts to understand these difficulties through drawings are just the first step in an effort to get into the problem. They make no pretense at an attempt to find "The Solution" to the child's problems in the drawings. The rapidity with which they go from case to case and the very style of writing about the child shows how this projective test, as well as others, should be used. The authors obviously use projective tests as adjuncts to interview and therapy techniques which can probe more deeply into the problems of the child and ultimately permit the weighing of alternative and sometimes incompatible hypotheses about the origin of the child's difficulties and the best management or intervention techniques. The authors' subtle sense of humor shows they also reject initial hypotheses and are well aware of the risk that interpretations of drawings without serious *independent* attempts to establish (validate) meanings can be quite misleading.

I feel almost apologetic about writing a heavy-handed introduction on the use of projective techniques in a foreword to this light, though deep, book. My only reason is that I have seen projective tools dreadfully misused in foolish hands. However, there is no protection whatever against such misuse. The very style of the book effectively instructs diagnosticians and therapists on the optimal use of projective materials, and leaves no doubt that the authors themselves use such material with exquisite selectivity. For the flexible, mature, non-doctrinaire clinician, therefore, this book harbors a gold mine of ideas and clearly shows how profound Anaxagoras was in linking the word "understanding" with the concept of "giving movement to previously inert elements." In brief, the reader should thoroughly enjoy this informative and valuable book.

Henry J. Mark, Sc.D.
*Department of Pediatrics*
*The Johns Hopkins School of Medicine*
*Baltimore, Maryland*

# CONTENTS

7

# PREFACE

This book is about children's human figure drawings. It proposes a new set of instructions to the child, namely to draw everyone in the family *doing* something. These kinetic (action) drawings have been found to be more informative than drawings obtained by the traditional akinetic instructions.

We have been gathering kinetic family drawings for about eleven years and found them so helpful in understanding troubled children that we decided to share this experience through this book.

The "idea" for seriously gathering kinetic drawings was stumbled upon by one of us eleven years ago. At that time he was attempting to trace the origin of the word "intelligence." (2) This quest eventually led to the dawning of the "golden age" of Greece and to Anaxagoras of Clazomenae (500-428 B.C.). Few are familiar with the works (mostly fragments) of Anaxagoras as they are with his student, Socrates, or with those of Socrates' student, Plato. Most of us know Socrates drank hemlock, but few know he was forced to drink hemlock for espousing the views of Anaxagoras.

Among the Greeks, Anaxagoras was known as ho NOUS (*the* understanding). Ionian science was introduced into Athens by Anaxagoras who "was the first philosopher to take up his resi-

9

dence in Athens, which was then making itself, under the leadership of Pericles, the most prominent city in Greece." (15)

Anaxagoras defined understanding (NOUS) as, "*Giving movement, unity and system to what had previously been a jumble of inert elements.*" This seemed at the time (and still does) the most comprehensive definition of the process of "intellectualizing" ever stated.

In any event, having been enamored by the work of Anaxagoras, it seemed self-evident that to "understand" children we must give them tasks involving movement, i.e., kinetic instructions. From this ancient beginning, some 10,000 kinetic family drawings (K-F-D) were collected by us. Sixty K-F-D's are presented here as representative of our collection.

We are grateful to the Children's Orthopedic Hospital and Medical Center, Seattle, Washington, for its loving care and atmosphere, which provided a haven for the troubled children producing most of our pictures. Our thanks to Miss Nancy Walton and Mrs. Borg Wagner for their tireless efforts in preparing the manuscript and to Mrs. Ada Pepin, who so skillfully and enthusiastically prepared and photographed the drawings.

Our thanks, naturally, to the children who produced the K-F-D's. The drawings were often so "dynamic" they left the authors groping for words to express that which the child had expressed so well with a few strokes of a pencil.

# KINETIC
# FAMILY
# DRAWINGS
## (K-F-D)

# 1

# INTRODUCTION

Young children usually express themselves more naturally and spontaneously through actions rather than through words. Thus, figure drawing provides an excellent method of exploring the world of the child. Drawing tests are simple to administer, nonthreatening, and can be used where other techniques are limited by such factors as language barrier, cultural deprivation, and inability to communicate.

Children's drawings can be analyzed in a number of ways. Recently Di Leo (4) has written a book discussing children's art from the pediatrician's view, with emphasis on normal developmental as well as deviant characteristics. Kellogg's (9) current work describes the mental development of children as reflected in their art. The recent comprehensive work of Koppitz (10) focuses on children's drawings as related to school achievement. Thus, the Human Figure Drawings of children may be obtained using a variety of instructions and methods of analysis.

*Analysis of Human Figure Drawings as a Psychological Test:*

In 1926, Florence Goodenough published "Measurement of Intelligence by Drawings." (5) The child was asked to "Draw a person," (D-A-P), and the drawing was scored for mental age. The scoring was done by adding up the points given for inclusion of parts, i.e., head, arms, feet, fingers, etc. The Goodenough D-A-P test quickly became an accepted and widely used psychological test of intelligence.

In 1948, Buck introduced the house-tree-person (H-T-P) technique. (1) The child was asked to draw a house, a tree, and a person and clinical interpretations of the drawing were made. Buck felt the test aided the clinician in obtaining information concerning the sensitivity, maturity, flexibility, and degree of personality integration through analysis of the person. The house and tree provide additional information concerning the growth (tree) and environmental feelings (house) of the patient. The H-T-P was one of the first uses of human figure drawings as a psychological projective test.

Karen Machover's book, "Personality Projection in the Drawing of the Human Figure," published in 1949, discussed some of the qualitative aspects related to psychopathology in human figure drawings. (11)

Analysis of a single figure drawing may prove revealing as shown in Figure A. One doesn't have to know much about psychological tests to feel that the boy who produced this drawing is "bound-up." It is less obvious to determine the meaning of the expression in the face, which may be distress or a smiling denial of the "bound-up" features of the upper body, or even comfort and security in having his impulses controlled.

14

Figure A

# KINETIC FAMILY DRAWINGS (K-F-D)

For readers not familiar with Machover's work, a summary of some of the characteristics of individual human figure drawings and their clinical interpretation is outlined.

*Some Characteristics of Individual Human Figure Drawings and Their Meaning:*

1. *Shading or scribbling:*
   Shading in a drawing suggests preoccupation, fixation, and anxiety.

2. *Buttons:*
   Emphasis on buttons suggests dependency.

3. *Long necks:*
   This distortion is related to dependency.

4. *Facial expression:*
   Expressions depicting various emotions were felt to be one of the more reliable signs, according to Machover.

5. *Exaggeration of body parts:*
   Enlargement or exaggeration of bodily parts suggests preoccupation with the function of those parts. For example, enlarged ears suggests preoccupation with being able to hear.

6. *Omission of body parts:*
   Omission of body parts often indicates denial of its function.

7. *Size:*
   Size of a drawing suggests a diminished or exaggerated

view of that person. The person who feels very inadequate usually draws a tiny person.

8. *Cross-hatching:*
This sign suggests "controlled" shading and is related to obsessive thoughts.

9. *Precise Drawing:*
Orderliness, neatness, and precision in a drawing often reflect a child's concern or needs for a structured environment. Overconcern with structure may be viewed as an attempt to control a threatening environment.

10. *Pressure:*
The pressure used in producing a drawing suggests outward or inward direction of impulse, i.e., the depressed person presses lightly; the aggressive, acting-out individual uses excessive pressure.

These are examples of the more frequent characteristics of individual human drawings.

In 1951, Hulse discussed some aspects of conflict expressed in drawing a family, (D-A-F). (7, 8) Use of the D-A-F has been discussed by Reznikoff (14) and Di Leo (4).

All of the aforementioned psychological tests use akinetic instructions; children are asked to draw a person or draw a house-tree-person, or draw a family. While useful information may be obtained, akinetic instructions usually result in relatively static, rigid drawings.

The approach of using kinetic (action) instructions, i.e., asking the child to produce a drawing where figures were *moving* or doing something, has been found to produce much more valid and dynamic material in the attempt to understand the psychopathology of children in a family setting.

# 2

# COMPARISON OF

# KINETIC AND AKINETIC

# DRAWINGS

This book aims to improve our *understanding* of children through analysis of their kinetic family drawings, (K-F-D).

*Procedure:*

The drawings are obtained from children individually, not in group sessions. The child is asked to seat himself on a small chair at a table of appropriate height. A sheet of plain white, 11″ by 8 1/2″ paper is placed on the table directly in front of him. A pencil (No. 2) is placed in the center of the paper and he is asked to:

"Draw a picture of everyone in your family, including you, *doing* something. Try to draw whole people, not cartoons or stick people. Remember, make everyone *doing* something—some kind of action."

The examiner then leaves the room and checks periodically. The situation is terminated when the child indicates verbally or by gesture that he has finished. No time limit is made. Noncompliance is extremely rare. If the child says, "I can't," he is encouraged periodically and left in the room until completion of the K-F-D.

*Comparison of D-A-P, H-T-P, D-A-F, and K-F-D:*

Akinetic instructions, such as "Draw-A-Person" or "Draw-A-Family," yield relatively inert figures. The drawings of the same individual show remarkable consistency over a period of time. Machover observed that such drawings bear the consistency of a signature.

The drawings of Chris, a 13-year-old girl, brought to the hospital for various complaints, such as headaches, fainting and abdominal pains, will help demonstrate the relative value of the kinetic family drawing, (K-F-D).

Figure B shows the traditional drawing when Chris was asked to draw a person.

Obviously, this drawing shows Chris to have good intelligence. But even more, if we look for it, we can begin to see certain personality characteristics. The preciseness of the drawing suggests compulsivity, even to the extent that the child seems to overcompensate with the design of the blouse being off-center. One wonders also about sexual ambivalence in the "pants-skirt," and the two-dimensional or flat bosom.

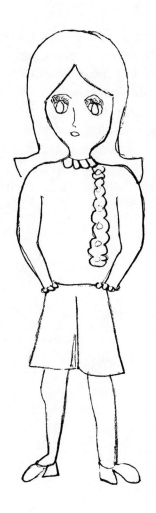

DRAW-A-PERSON

Figure B

Figure C shows Chris's drawing of a house-tree-person.

The analysis of the H-T-P includes the size of the tree, chimney, door, etc. However, in terms of "understanding" and alleviating Chris's symptoms, this drawing proved of little value. But unanswered hints of deeper problems appeared in the H-T-P drawings; for example, the reappearance of compulsive balancing in the drawing of the house, the question mark doorhandle, and the economical use of the side of the house as the left side of the tree trunk, which makes them intertwined and united. One cannot leave this drawing without seeing that the child is still wearing pants, but is beginning to have other female sexual characteristics.

HOUSE-TREE-PERSON

Figure C

Figure D shows Chris's drawing of a family when using the verbal instructions of Hulse, that is, to Draw a Family.

Chris's drawing of the family is a relatively rigid, stylized group of individual figures. The crosshatching on the "self" suggest obsessive thoughts and concerns. Nevertheless, in spite of the rigidity of the family, more of the dynamics of the child's problems begin to show. The father's face is pockmarked. His eyes are the least expressive of anyone's in the family. The women—mother, older sister and the patient—begin to be modified by their sexuality. Both mother and older sister have two pockets in the areas of the breasts that reveal their sexuality. But interestingly enough, the patient, whose sexuality is of deep concern, by the crosshatching, actually crosses out and once again denies her sexuality.

DRAW-A-FAMILY

Figure D

# KINETIC FAMILY DRAWINGS (K-F-D)

Chris was asked to draw a picture of everyone in her family doing something. The results are shown in Figure 1.

When asked to produce a kinetic drawing, Chris became somewhat uneasy. Her first question was, "Can I put them in separate rooms?" She proceeded to compartmentalize herself and worked to enclose and isolate her father. Father's face is turned away in contrast to the other members of the family. Note the maze the father must follow, past the mother, up the winding stairs to Chris and past Chris to the three younger children. More than that, we have some interesting speculative observations. There is a reversal of roles with father working at the stove in the kitchen, while mother is in the living room smoking a cigarette. One also wonders about the tiny chairs around the table, almost as if the child is denying the anatomical part necessary to sit on. Further, in spite of the circuitous course that the figure of father must travel to get to mother and finally to the last room, it is interesting that the child isolates herself in her bedroom where she could eventually be found by father and be fairly well insulated from the rest of the family.

Chris had been removed from her family, as had the other children, because of the father's problems. According to the mother, he had sexually molested all of the children and was institutionalized for sexual molestation. Chris, in her K-F-D, gives

Figure 1

us a good deal of the dynamics within this family and her attempts to isolate herself from the very threatening father.

The D-A-P, H-T-P, and D-A-F methods gave us some hints in understanding Chris. The K-F-D improved our understanding of Chris: once we "understood," we could help her.

# 3

# KINETIC

# FAMILY

# DRAWINGS

In Chapter 1, we discussed some of the characteristics of individual drawings and their interpretation. The analysis of kinetic drawing focuses on the action or movement rather than the inert figures.

*Some Characteristics of K-F-D's and Their Meaning:*

A. *Styles:*

1. *Compartmentalization:*
   Children attempt to isolate themselves (and their feelings) from other family members through compartmentalizing.

2. *Underlining:*
Drawing a line across the bottom of the page is characteristic of children from unstable families.

B. *Actions:*

1. *Mother:*
   a. *Cooking:* This is the most frequent action of mother in K-F-D and reflects a mother figure who meets the child's nurturant needs.
   b. *Cleaning:* This action is found in compulsive mothers who are more preoccupied with the house than with the people in the house. Cleaning becomes equated to acceptable or good behavior.
   c. *Ironing:* Usually found in the overly involved mother trying too hard to give her child "warmth."

2. *Fathers:*
   a. *Household activities:* Reading the paper, paying the bills, playing with the kids, are frequent activities of normal dads.
   b. *Driving to or at work:* Usually found in fathers who are thought of in terms of abandonment or being outside of the family, rather than an integral part of it.
   c. *Cutting:* Activities such as mowing the lawn, chopping, cutting, etc. are seen with "tough" or "castrating" fathers. (Occasionally mothers.)

3. *Rivalry:*
Usually depicted as a force or action between members of the family, i.e., throwing a ball, knife, airplane, etc. Seen in highly competitive or "jealous" children.

These are a few of the common "actions" that frequently re-appear in the K-F-D.

A characteristic mental disturbance in Freud's day was the anxiety-hysteria now seen relatively infrequently.

Mary, a 12-year-old girl, was brought to the hospital with a reported history of recent rape by her brother. Mary's kinetic drawing is shown in Figure 2.

Note the intensity of the scribbling on Mary's body. She shows a great preoccupation in this area and obvious concern and distortion in her drawing. This reflects her own concern about her body and her great anxiety in reaction to the rape episode. Further, the scribbling or "blacking out" gives us another feeling of the dynamics involved in which Mary attempts at the same time to deny the existence of her sexuality.

Note also the brother in this drawing. His body is cut off below the waist by the chair. This is another technique used by children in terms of denying or repressing areas and an inability to "think" about these areas.

Mary's drawing is characteristic of anxiety-hysteria in children and is a form well-known traditionally through Freud's work with hysteria.

Self

Mother

Dad

Brother

Figure 2

More characteristic of the psychopathology of the children we see is the type of kinetic style shown in Figure 3.

Mike, who produced this drawing, is a 17-year-old boy, brought to the hospital because of withdrawal symptoms. His father had a history of a car accident, with a head injury and being extremely irritable subsequent to this. Mike felt completely isolated and rejected by the father. Note in the drawing the compartmentalization. This is a method that children use to isolate themselves from people and to deny feeling. Note the distance between Mike and the father in the drawing and his turning to the refrigerator for nurturance, rather than to people; even mother, although in the kitchen, has her back turned.

Although it is not our purpose to attempt to develop prognostic or therapeutic availability indications from these drawings, it is interesting to take note of some factors in Mike's drawing in this regard.

This young man became a patient of one of us, and although the results of treatment could be measured as "successful" because some of the crippling symptoms of underachievement, isolation, and social withdrawal diminished, certain character factors remained unchanged.

He felt father preferred the older brother and would only approve of Mike if Mike was "good." Mother was always there and providing necessities, but in a detached neutral way, and was a warm person only when playing the role of "mother." He was afraid of his brother and felt isolated from his sisters. It was difficult for him to say that he felt rejected, but it was also apparent that he has always felt rejected and continued to do so. In early adolescence the parents uprooted him and sent him to several different boarding schools, where he continued to underachieve,

Figure 3

act out in covert delinquency and always felt shy and unattractive. His close friends were primarily among the fringe delinquent groups in the home neighborhood and at school.

All this is so well demonstrated and predicted in his drawing —the separation by compartmentalization, the "cutting" brother, the isolation from the parents and sisters, and even the "stealing" food (love) from the cold refrigerator.

The beginning of this type of isolation in children is shown in Figure 4.

Mark A., a 10-year-old boy, was brought in for evaluation of his withdrawal tendencies and his general anxieties.

His drawing shows the shading of the area below the sister. The boy has a great rivalry with this sister and anger directed toward her. This preoccupation is seen clearly in the kinetic drawing. Also, the increased withdrawal of the boy is concretely seen in his building a fence around himself, as well as compartmentalizing the drawing.

The kinetic dynamics in Figure 4 so characterize the factors involved in Mark A.'s withdrawal and his general anxieties, that one must mention not only the compartmentalization, but also the extent of these lines running from the bottom to the top of the page with almost no chance of contaminating one compartment with the other. The steam from the boiling pot is caught and segregated in the hood overhanging the stove. The grass-cutting, castrating father, the fear of the striving little brother on stilts, and the thinly veiled hostility toward the drowning sister are all finally capped with the converging strong fence that protects him from all of this.

This withdrawal from people and the feeling of being isolated and depersonalized is very characteristic of many of the drawings of our children and perhaps characteristic of the psychopathology of our time, just as anxiety-hysteria was characteristic of Freud's time.

36

Figure 4

# 4

# IDENTIFICATION

# AND EARLY

# EMOTIONAL DEPRIVATION

Identification is a part of growth and development. It is an essential portion of character formation. This is usually an automatic or unconscious process and parents or parent surrogates are the earliest objects of this identification, as well as siblings and others as they are added to the child's environment. Figure 5 shows a little girl who loves her daddy and one can only conjecture about the closeness of the relationship.

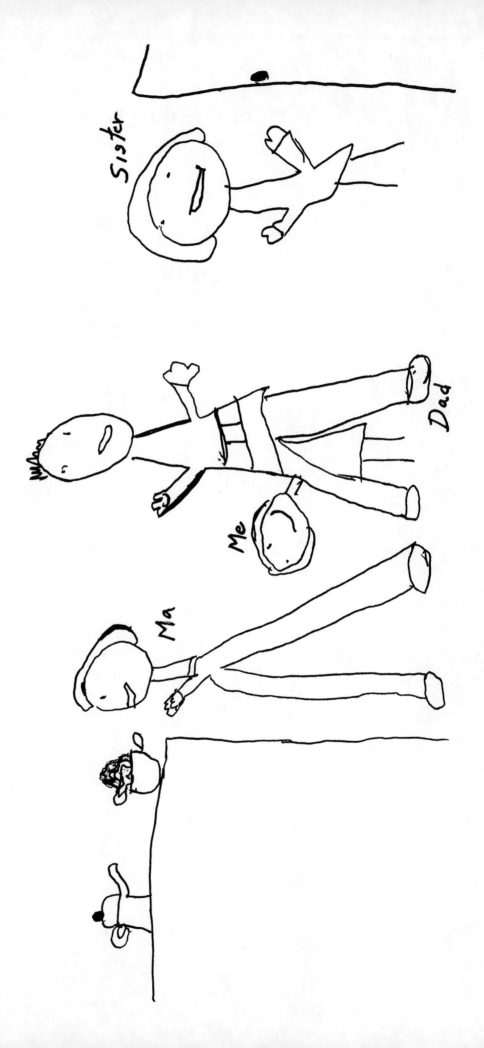

Figure 5

Sometimes a new baby comes along and drives children close to the parents, as in Figure 6.

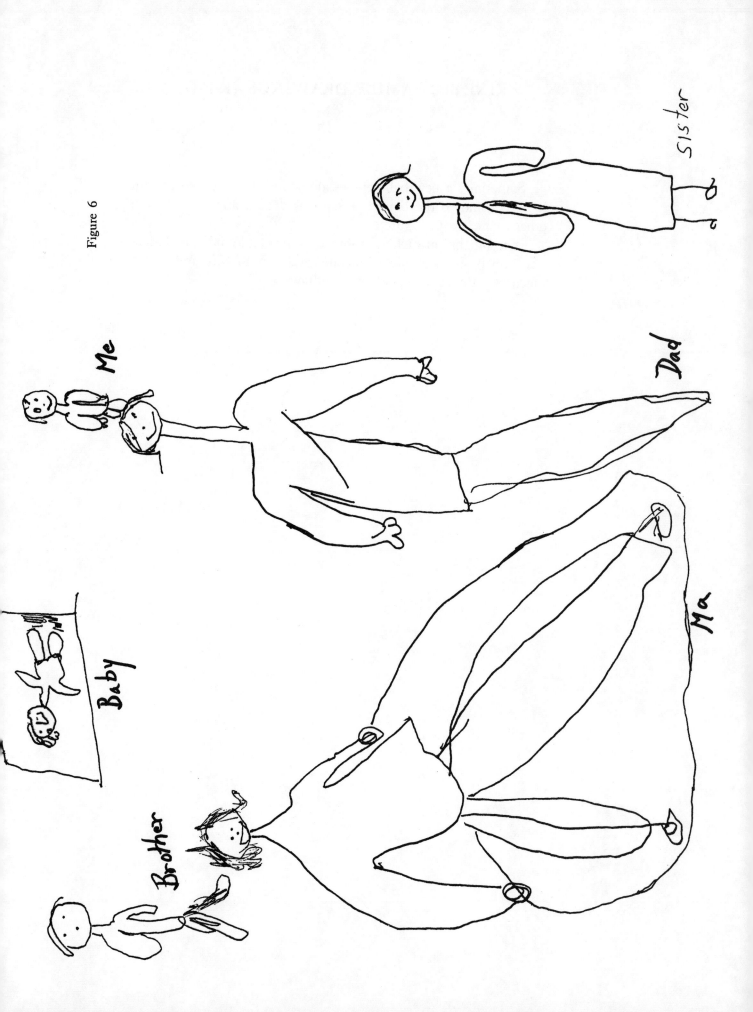

Figure 6

Sometimes a new baby comes along and it is just too painful to accept and so the baby's presence is denied and he's "in the other room," as in Figure 7.

It seems that in such an instance, comfortable individual identification is so incomplete that any addition to this unit is too much of a threat to include in the drawing.

Figure 7

"Baby is in the other room"

Some children never have a parent with whom they can get close or feel real emotional empathy.

Dave was an 8-year-old boy brought in for evaluation of his unending demands for "attention." He tended to act up in the lunchroom at school and to always be seeking the mother's attention. If she did not give it to him, he became very angry.

Dave was adopted at 6 months of age. Prior to this, he had been in five different foster homes and apparently deprived, according to the history. The pediatrician had told the mother to keep the boy at home for several months because of his general fears and unusual history.

Dave's 11-year-old brother had been adopted at four days of age and was normal, according to the parents.

Dave's drawing of the family is shown in Figure 8.

When Dave started this drawing, he began with a chicken on the table, then came the brother eating the chicken and finally Dave, unable to quite reach the food.

Note the similarities in Figure 8 to those shown in Figure 2, with the shading. In this case, the shading is below the father, who is depicted as a stove. Everyone in the family is involved in eating. The repetition of the stars reflects the obsessive thoughts of the boy.

Figure 8

The obsessive thoughts with food are repeated in Figure 9.

Figure 9 was drawn by a 9-year-old boy with a history of severe deprivation the first few years of life. He drew himself close to the mother and the stomach area shows obsessive preoccupations, as reflected in the position of the geometric designs in the table-cloth. One cannot leave this drawing without mentioning the father, the only non-stick figure, with his full mouth of teeth, his "big belly," his cutting-carving implements and his obsessionally, ominously, spotted feet.

Figure 9

DAD CUTTING MEAT
MOTHER DISHING UP VEGETABLES
Sister (17)
Sister (13)
Sister (3)
Me (9)

This theme is repeated in Figure 10, with a 14-year-old girl brought to the hospital because of severe abdominal pains. She had preoccupations with being fed and a history of emotional deprivation. An interesting observation in view of this is that there are no eating utensils before the patient, only flowers. (The symbols of growth and love?) Also, in the position at the table she is farthest from the source of food (parental love).

12-18-43

Dad    Mom    Sharon    ME
                          (14)

Figure 10

Figure 11 is that of a 12-year-old boy, hospitalized for severe ulcerative colitis. He has a history of severe emotional deprivation because of a depressed mother in the first year of life. The mother is depicted as a stove and the nurturance he gets from her is all-important in his life. For the first time the vacuum cleaner appears and in relation to this deprived boy, with a pathological intestine. This drawn symbol appears repeatedly in children with a history of oral deprivation.

Figure 11

Again in Figure 12 one can see the preoccupation with the vacuum cleaner, as an intestinal symbol, so frequently seen in older children with a history of unmet dependency needs. This is a K-F-D by a 17-year-old child.

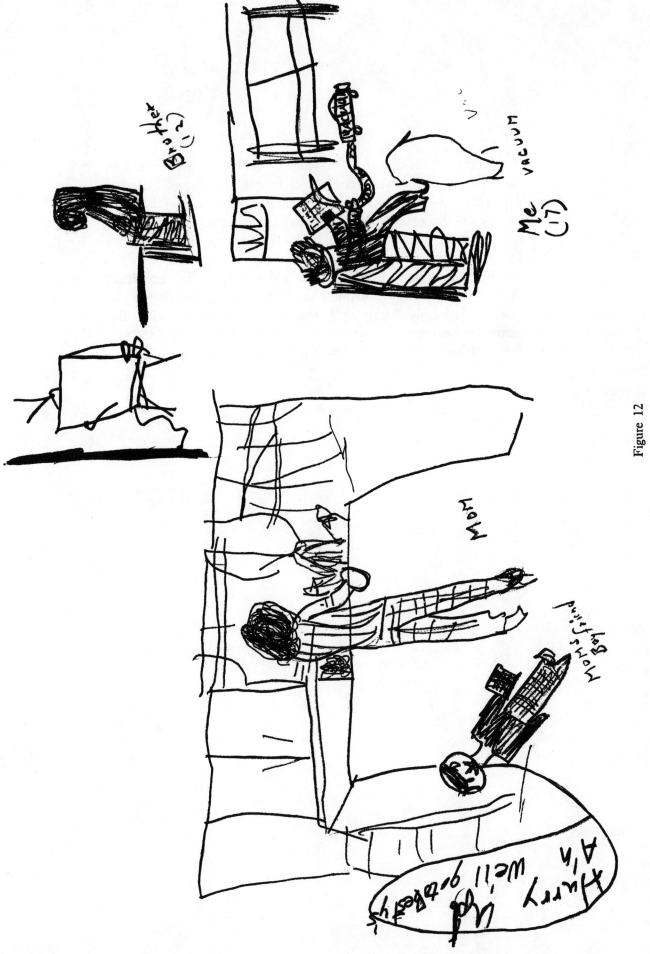

Figure 12

Figure 13 was drawn by 16-year-old Tim. His mother was an alcoholic, usually down at the corner tavern. Because of maternal deprivation Tim was driven to run through life seeking that illusive "butterfly of love" and denying the painful existence of a non-mothering mother. Tim had about given up seeking mother love. Tim was also dying of severe "intractable" asthma.

It seems almost superfluous to add words to this exquisite, dynamic drawing. The inability to express direct hostility to the mother, but only "drawing her absent," and substituting the search for beauty in the form of the butterfly as displaced destructive hostility is done much better in drawing than in words.

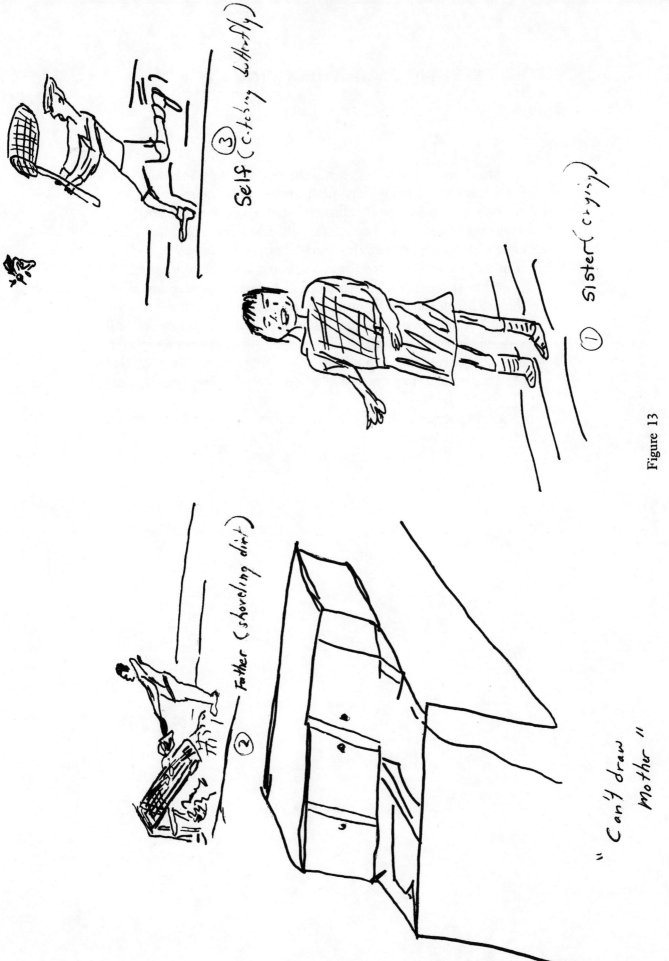

③ Self (catching butterfly)

① Sister (crying)

② Father (shoveling dirt)

"Can't draw mother"

Figure 13

The foregoing drawing demonstrates the ways in which the K-F-D can reveal many dynamic features, using components and symbols that begin to be characteristic of passive-aggressive behavior, of serious emotional, especially oral deprivations, and the child's frustrated demands for parental attention and love. Timing is important and most of these children given the test suffer deprivation very early when the oral or nutrient relationship with the mother or mother figure is the paramount need in the child's life. The mother's post-partum depression, post-partum medical or surgical problems that necessitated maternal infant separation over a prolonged period of time, and psychological rejection of the child are some of the maternal characteristics seen in the foregoing life histories.

Further exploration of identification problems will be demonstrated in the next section.

# 5

# PROBLEMS OF

# IDENTIFICATION

# IN GIRLS

In the growing identification during latency, most girls strive to be as beautiful and desirable as the female figures with whom they are identifying. This normal character development may be interfered with by neurotic conflict such as difficulty in resolution of the Oedipal situation, or more than the usual ambivalence toward the identifiable object.

The projection of this critical process is so universal that the problems around it are seen in the fairy tales of different cultures, for example, Snow White, Cinderella, Beauty and the Beast, etc. In these stories, the girl is striving for her identification, is recognized as beautiful, has mixed feelings about herself, but emerges in the end the lovely and beautiful sexual partner of a handsome prince. This is accomplished, however, only after traversing the dangerous forest of the vengeful and destructive mother, or of other females who, of course, are rivals. For example, Cinderella is taken by the good mother (the fairy godmother) to the Ball, despite the stepmother and stepsisters who refused to let her attend.

It is Cinderella who wins the prince, after much travail, while the stepmother and stepsisters are defeated in their quest for the reward of femininity. It is important also to point out that in almost all of these stories the direct hostility is toward stepmothers, witches, stepsisters, or others to camouflage the unacceptable hostility toward the real mother and real siblings.

Cathy, an 11-year-old girl, who produced the drawing in Figure 14, captures the central theme in many girls' drawings. She makes herself an idealized type of beauty. In reality, Cathy is a very homely girl while her sister, Vickie, is very pretty. The little girl's wish fulfillment and clenched fist directed toward her sister poignantly reflects her desire to outshine her rival.

Girls assume an adult feminine role through identification with a mother figure. Numerous problems often prevent adequate identification.

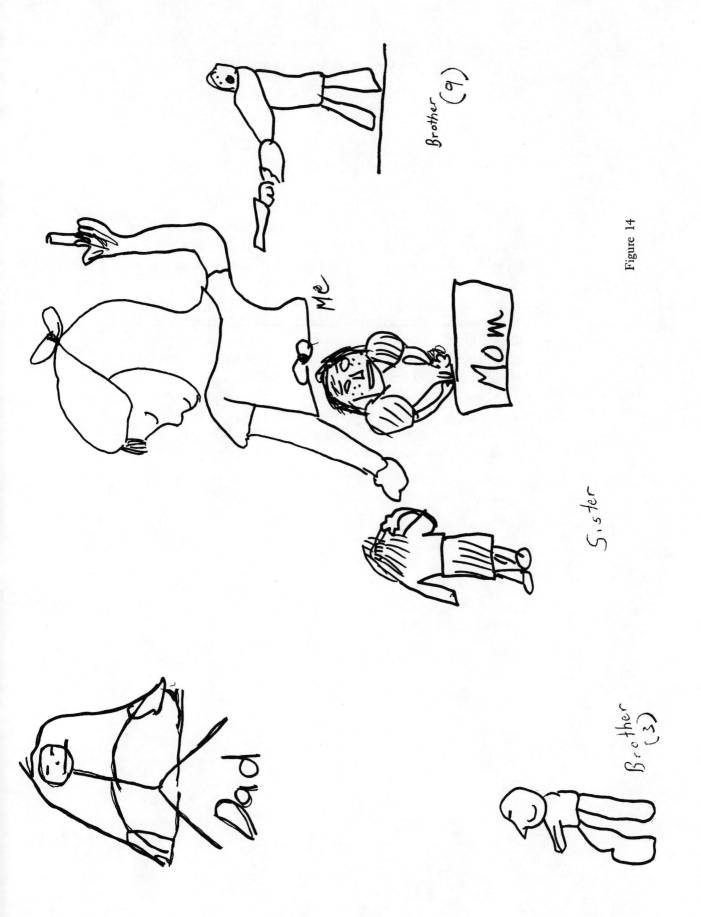

Brother (9)

Me

Mom

Sister

Dad

Brother (3)

Figure 14

*Common Problems in Girls' Identifications with Mother:*

### A. THE OVERPOWERING AND DOMINANT MOTHER

Figure 15 shows the drawing of Nancy, a little 9-year-old girl with an overly close or symbiotic relationship to the mother. The mother was a very successful business woman who overpowered and dominated her family. This is an example of genuine identity confusion. If the child identifies with the feminized or weak father, she would of course run the risk of being rejected by the mother as he is. However, to identify with the mother, she would of course have to relinquish her femininity, as the mother has hers. So the child, in her confusion and her paralyzing ambivalence, remains symbiotically tied to the mother and development remains static. It is interesting to point out further that in this case, as in every one, development is not really static, but goes on. In the case of Nancy, serious somatic symptoms developed.

Dad

Mu

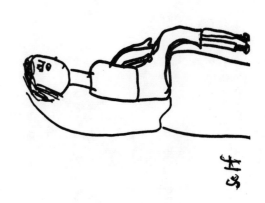

Self

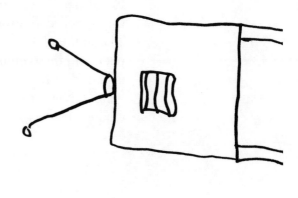

Figure 15

### B. THE SEDUCTIVE MOTHER

Sometimes a girl has a mother who is very seductive and with whom competition is difficult, if not impossible. Gayle, a 15-year-old girl, was brought to the hospital because of her dreams and fears that something might happen to the mother. The drawing in Figure 16 shows her preoccupation with the mother and the girl's thinly veiled destructive wishes. Her ambivalence is paramount. The figure of the mother is the best-drawn figure. Details are explicit and the femininity is without question. However, the mother is placed in the most vulnerable of all positions. She is seductively lying on her back, but is exposed to the lawn mower, to the croquet mallets and ball, and even to the sun.

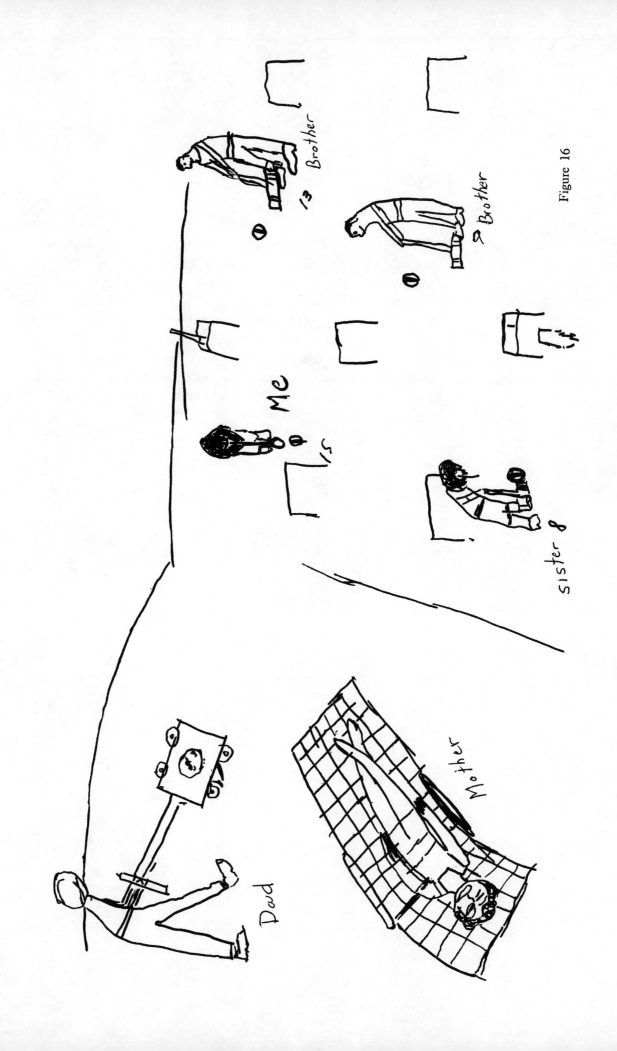

Figure 16

### C. THE "TOMBOY"

Some little girls are brought up in families where males predominate, as in the case of 11-year-old Robin, in Figure 17. While she is close to the mother, she does tend to identify with boys' activities and is characterized as a "tomboy." The light bulbs surrounding the brother, father and herself appear to be phallic symbols. The parents are concerned about Robin's excessive "boyishness." The brothers may indeed have been the favorites in the family; the mother unimportant. Though Robin is 11 years old, the Oedipus situation in girls is notoriously longer lasting than in boys and she may still be struggling for father's favor, only to feel that the father will accept her more if she is more "boyish."

Figure 17

*Identification of Girls in Adolescence:*

At puberty and in early adolescence many girls "love" horses. When questioned about their reasons for loving horses they state simply, "They're the most beautiful animal and people can ride them." Girls at this age not only love horses, but they identify with horses and occasionally are horses, as shown in Figure 18. The safe comfortable sexual symbolic identification seems universal in western culture.

Figure 18

Lori, a 15-year-old girl who is quite normal, has been competing with the mother in attempting to grow up. Figure 19 clearly demonstrates how the girl handles this problem by identifying with the nurturant aspects of the mother, but cutting off her control (head).

Lori has "worked through" the problem of identification by first being the mother and then substituting her own controls for those of "mom."

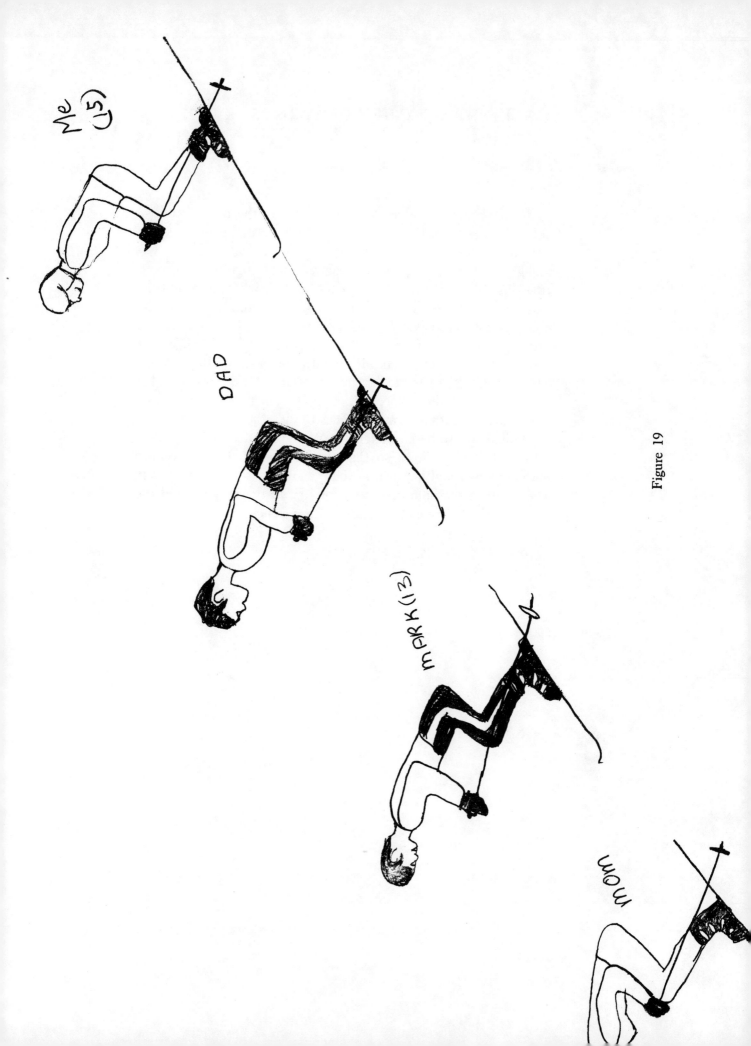

Figure 19

Many girls are unable to "work through" the normal process of identification and frequently present complicated neurotic symptoms associated with this inability. Kris, an 18-year-old girl, was brought to the hospital because of recurrent nightmares of cats attacking her. Kris was a very beautiful girl, who was voted the most popular in her high school class. Her mother, in contrast, was very much overweight and rather homely. However, in her drawing, shown in Figure 20, Kris tends to deny her own beauty and to attribute all the beautiful characteristics to the mother. The cat actually seems to be an extension of the mother and is characteristic of the preoccupation with cats that we have seen in girls having extreme ambivalences toward the mother.

This may also be characteristic of a resurgence of Kris's unresolved Oedipal feelings, so that her destructive hostile feelings toward mother and her own anxiety about her sexuality may very well result in the de-sexualization of Kris in the drawing and the overcompensatory characteristics of the mother.

Figure 20

# 6

# PROBLEMS OF

# IDENTIFICATION

# IN BOYS

In healthy intrafamily relationships, sexual identification is an accepted process from birth. The attitudes of members of the family, as well as of anyone and everyone in contact with the family, are a projection of masculinity toward the infant male. It is important to point out that these attitudes are based on those individuals' concepts of their own personalized identification styles. The projection of those very personalized attitudes is a continual process so that by about the third year the child begins genuine identification. So we can readily see that even this early identification is dependent on the health and adequacy of those most important to the child.

It is in this identification striving that the male child identifies with the older and stronger male family members, and also, because of the ambivalent nature of the relationship, including the need to remain dependent on mother, that competition for her love becomes a factor in intrafamily relationships.

In more or less healthy family constellations, mother maintains her relationship to father and thereby allows the son to find a genuine separate identification. However, in pathological instances, especially with the over-involved mothers, there is a division of the identification process.

The foregoing process is an essential part of what Freud called the Oedipal process, seeing a similarity in it to that of the ancient myth in the Greek family triangle tragedy, Oedipus Rex. It is obvious then that the process was not a theory in itself and that this developmental procedure was well known in the observances of man for generations and eras antedating the 19th Century.

Biologically, an Oedipal-like process is seen in sub-human species as well. The competition and aggressiveness of the young males results in establishing new family territories and selection survival. Carpenter's work with the great apes (3) has demonstrated this exquisitely in the case of gibbons. In this species, the aged male parent is finally defeated in the sense of the triangle struggle and the newest and strongest son replaces him.

Figure 21 shows a boy at the height of this stage at age 7. Note in the drawing that he has separated his mother and himself from the other males, who are far away in the drawing with a building in between. He and the mother are interacting in a growth process and the boy has "captured" the mother from the other males.

One can speculate, of course, in Figure 21 about the patient's preoccupation and anxiety around this struggle. One notes the long, phallic hose with which he captures his mother and which emits a fluid (water) into the hole "for the plant" (generation) and the large, phallic-like nosed sun, which shines approvingly (leeringly?) upon the scene.

Figure 21

This competitiveness is also reflected in Figure 22, drawn by a 7-year-old boy. The boy again is close to the mother and he and the father are engaged in an activity of planting. The mother is bringing a plant or beginning of life, and the boy is closest to her. Note the shading in the drawing, showing the boy's unconscious preoccupations in this area and the struggle with the male for the mother's love.

The fact that the generative plant theme is a frequent theme in the K-F-D gives some validity to the hypothetical impressions.

Figure 22

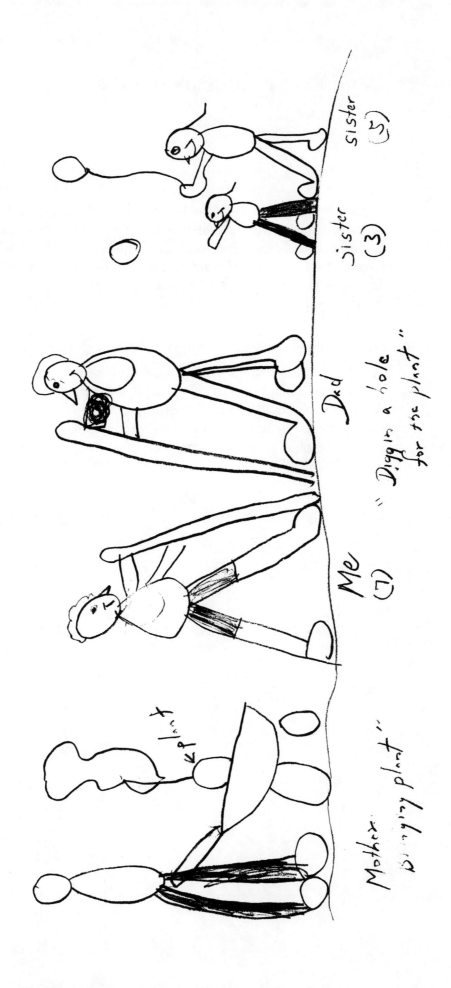

*Castration Fears*

The normal development in boys of competing with fathers or older brothers for the love of the female and attempting to be the dominant male can often be quite frightening to the boy. If perchance he has a very threatening or aggressive or destructive father, or if the older brother fits this role, then the boy's desire to be the strongest is unfulfilled and he becomes anxious about this competition.

Figure 23 shows an 8-year-old boy who is completely overwhelmed by the older brother. He has cut himself off at the neck and is threatened by the cutting tool, the lawnmower below him. This is a typical drawing of boys who, in the family setting, are fearful of the older males and fear castration.

Figure 23

This theme is repeated in the drawing of a 6-year-old boy shown in Figure 24. The father is a huge dominant person in the boy's life and he is very afraid of being hurt or castrated by the father. In the drawing we note that the boy is even afraid to draw his hands because he is afraid of losing extensions of the body. The anxiety is reflected again in the shading of the boy's body.

It is important to point out that the fear of castration or injury on the part of a younger male is not limited to the family settings where the father and older male siblings are necessarily hostile or destructive in their attitude toward the child, but rather the fact that he is younger, smaller, consciously and unconsciously competitive, and therefore vulnerable to the vengeful reaction of the objects of his competition. Further, the presence of the "cutting" older sib or father or the drawing of the "cut" self-figure, would depend not only on the pathology of the inter-personal relationships within the family, but on the timing or age of the child as it relates to the Oedipal situation.

Dad

Mom

Brother (11)

Me I wash my hands

Figure 24

Figure 25 perhaps most clearly demonstrates the castration fears. Randy, the boy who produced Drawing 25, has an alcoholic father who had a violent temper when he drank. The boy was unable to compete with him successfully. Notice the shading in the drawing, particularly the shading below the boy's waist. The father is "cutting" and has very obvious castration threats for this boy; also significant is the shape of father's "tool" and the shape of the object being cut.

Figure 25

*Ambivalence:*

In Figure 26, we see the action in a drawing of a fairly normal 8-year-old boy who is very competitive, however, and attempts to be the dominant person in the household. It is noted the two boys are in airplanes fighting and both competing with the father for the attention of the females in the family. Note that the father is on a ladder and falling, with a feeling of tension. The father is also carrying a lamp, which in many drawings is a symbol of love or warmth or sex.

This drawing reemphasizes the not-yet-resolved Oedipal situation and the conflicting ambivalence of the feeling for father who, while threatening, is also loving.

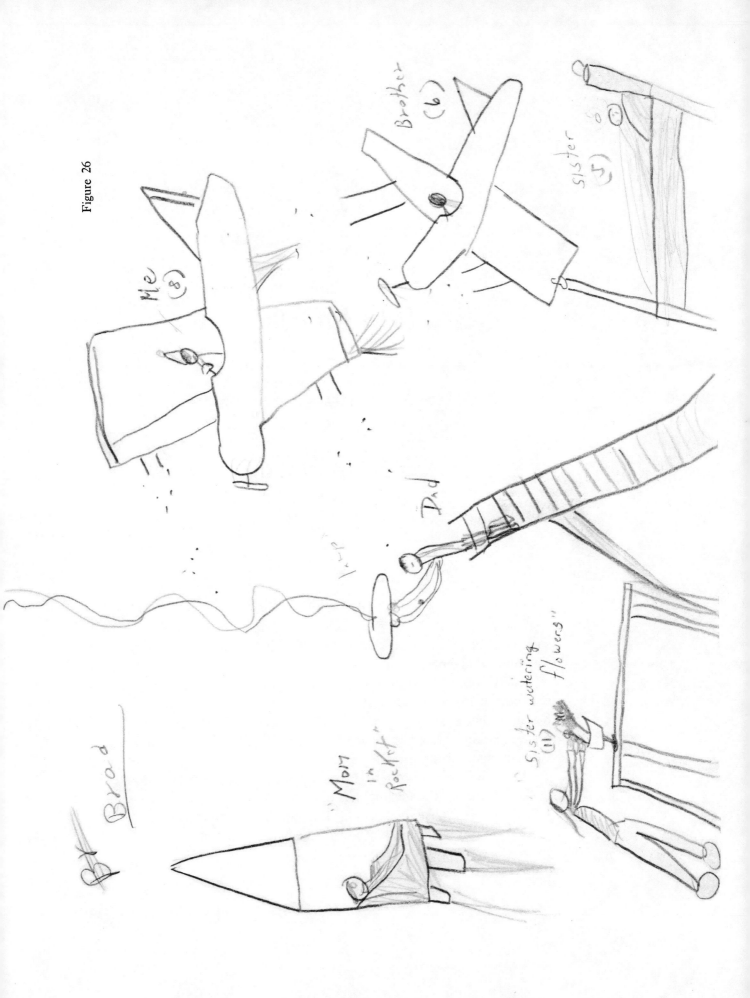

Figure 26

# 7

# THE LIGHT

# OR HEAT

# SYNDROME

The preoccupation with light or heat in many manifestations, such as light bulbs, fires, suns, or irons, will be seen throughout the family drawings.

The drawings of very young children give us some insight to the more complicated drawings of the older child. John was an 8-year-old boy who was brought in because of numerous fears and preoccupations. He was almost immobilized by these fears, being very shy and withdrawing.

The boy had a history of two surgeries on his penis because of the stricture of the meatus. His drawings reflect these anxieties. When asked to make his drawing, John started by obsessive criss-crossing in the top and bottom of the page and then made a

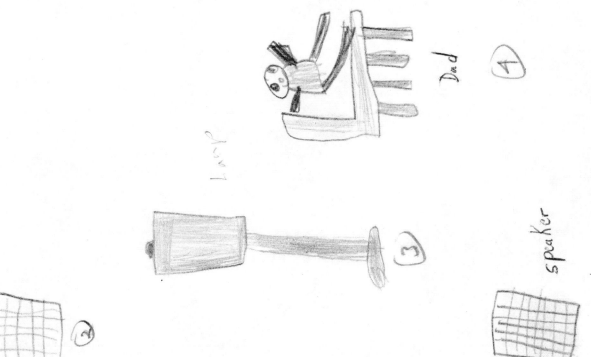

Figure 27

symbol of the lamp with a good deal of scribbling and anxiety. The lamp does have a penis-like shape and is a repetition of a theme seen frequently in drawings. The phallic-like extensions from all of the chairs and people are characteristic of the drawings of boys with severe castration fears.

Figure 28 was produced by a 9-year-old boy, with a history of emotional deprivation. Note the prominence of the lights in the center of the picture, reflecting the boy's need for warmth and love.

Figure 28

Perhaps the drawing of Mike, a 10-year-old boy seen because of numerous anxieties, more clearly depicts the light theme.

Mike was a boy who lived with the mother, a known prostitute. His K-F-D is seen in Figure 29. Mother had numerous men in the house and sexual activity was prominent and open and the boy saw much of this. The prominence of the three lights in the drawing reflects the intensity of this preoccupation in this home and family setting. The fact that the father was in prison and that the dog is protecting the boys from the ominous father is also part of the theme. The very significant underpinning in the drawing with the cross-hatching and the X-ing at the bottom is characteristic of a style in children where there is a great deal of instability in the family and the lining of the bottom of the page often reflects this yearning for stability. The low-hanging large bright lamps on their chains are indicative of the tremendous disturbance within this family, and also suggests that much of this disturbance has sexual overtones.

Figure 29

The intensity of the light theme and its relationship to the opposite sex is clearly depicted in Figure 30. Bill is a 10-year-old boy, whose father was killed two years previously. Bill is an only child and the very intense relationship between mother and son is reflected in the boy's drawing of the mother, who is encapsulated with the light above her while the boy is attached through her to numerous lights. The heat in the kitchen is intense, as seen in the steam and lights surrounding the encapsulated mother, Over and above this, of course, is the fact that the bulbs and phallic shapes of the lamps, with the boy holding onto them, continue the sexual theme.

Figure 30

Sharon, a very precocious 9-year-old girl, was brought to the hospital with the symptom of pulling out her eyelashes. Her family drawing is shown in Figure 31.

What is almost more significant here is what has been crossed out. The child depicts herself in her compartment as playing the violin, which is very acceptable and feminine. But the crossed-out figure would have had her tossing a ball to the brother who seems to be batting one with great vigor. Whether this kind of aggressive masculine behavior would have been too threatening to her one can only conjecture, especially since it is mother's displeasure that she fears.

The girl's symptoms began when the father left home on a trip. The girl was very much attached to him and very close to him. The intensity of the heat in this relationship is shown in the drawing of the father who is standing next to a fire in a phallic-like scene. Fire, then, is another frequent theme in K-F-D drawings.

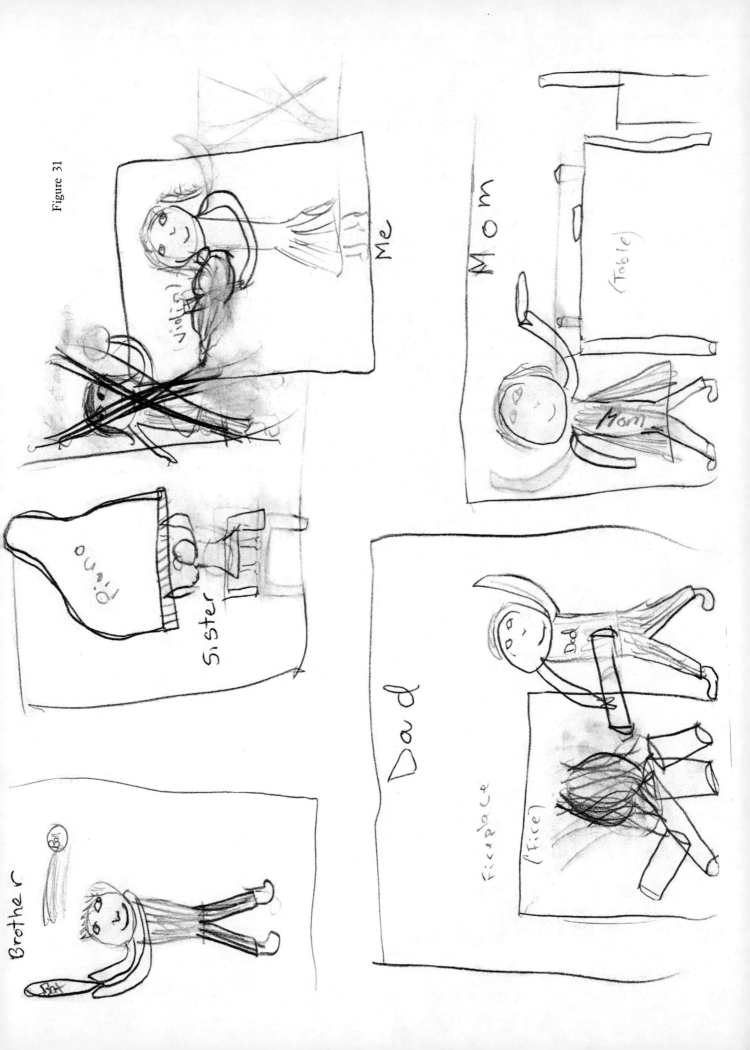

Figure 31

Lanny, a 14-year-old boy with a history of being placed in three foster homes and in great need for love and affection, produced the drawing in Figure 32.

The boy had established a relationship to the new foster mother and did derive some warmth and love from her. She, however, had a "nervous breakdown" and was taken from the family for a short time. The drawing of the figure of the mother, where she is encapsulated with the intensity of the light directed toward her, reflects the boy's need for warmth and love in this area. He feels rather as a social isolate, as indicated by the drawing, where he is faced away from the rest of the family. He derives a warmth in this family from the mother and the central picture of the mother with her encapsulation reflects this need. It is important to point out that only the mother is encapsulated and in the wish for the mother's love he has her sweeping away the cobwebs from the brightly shining, warm light of love. There is actually real dynamic wishing in this K-F-D.

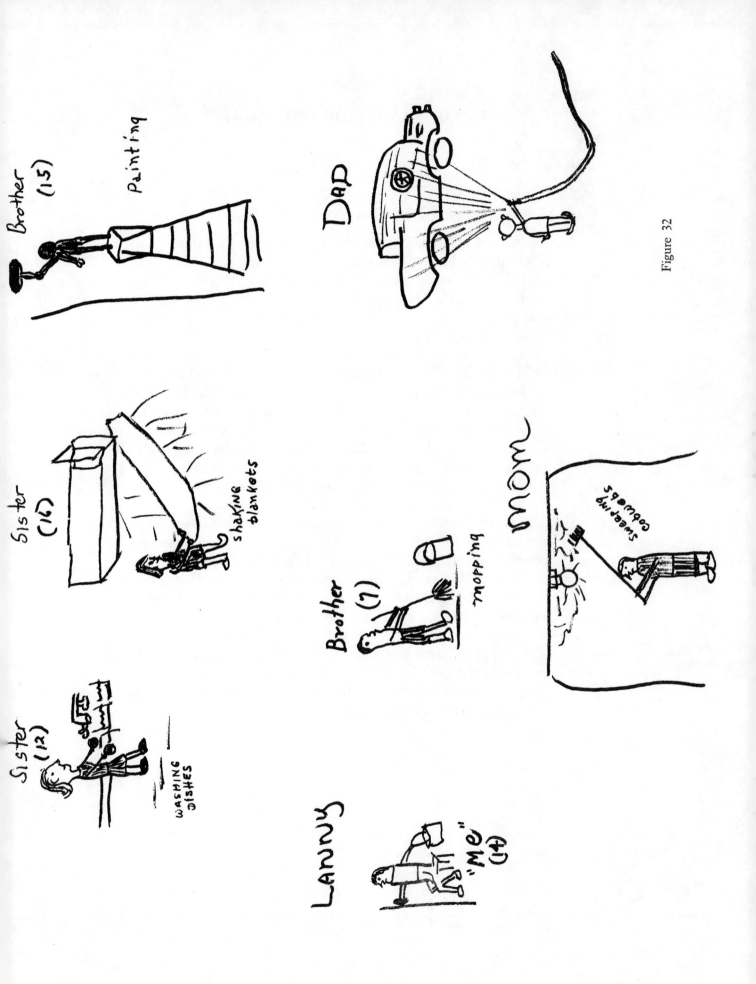

Figure 32

*The Ironing Board or "X" Syndrome*

In older children the intensity of the need for warmth and love reflected in the light and fire syndromes often brings about attempts at control of these emotions. This struggle for control was rather clearly depicted by Allan, a 16-year-old boy, who was brought in with great fears of staying home at certain times. Allan's drawing is shown in Figure 33.

In his drawing, Allan shades the area below the waist of the sister and mother, showing the usual preoccupation of adolescence in this area. In talking to Allan, utilizing clues from the K-F-D, it became clear that he was terrified if left alone with his rather seductive 11-year-old sister and abhorrent of any sexual impulse in this relationship. The controls are depicted by the girl holding her "stop" sign and by the young brother pointing a gun at him. The great attempts at control are seen in the "X" phenomena in the drawing. The table at which Allan sits is in the form of an "X" as is the container holding his food. The ironing board below the mother, with the "X" through the shaded area, is a constant theme with children attempting to control sexual impulse.

The significance of father racing away in his speedboat may be one of the underlying factors as to why the boy needs the number of external controls he depicts in the family drawing. Further, in view of the fact that this boy has only average intelligence within a family of superior intellectual and social achievement, one can also add that his frustrated anger is in the direction of acting out destructive or unacceptable impulse-ridden behavior in relation to the rest of the family.

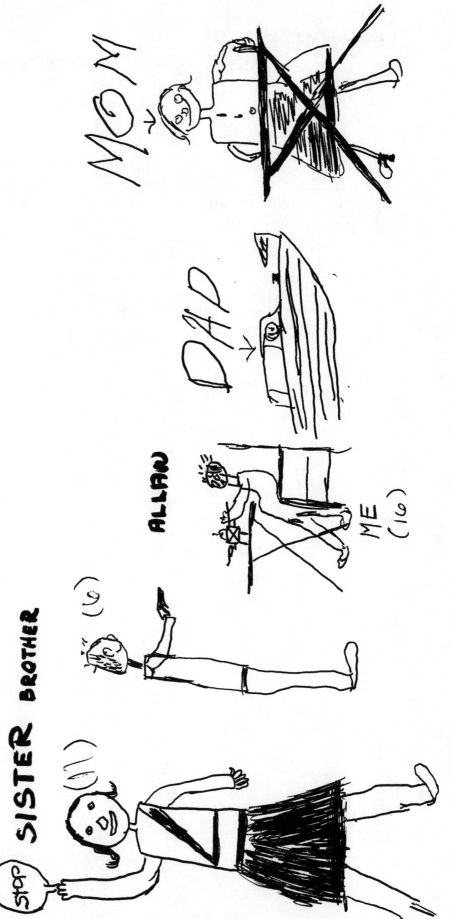

Figure 33

Dave's ironing board drawing is shown in Figure 34. This 12-year-old boy had lost his own mother from stomach cancer and was very much attracted to a stepmother, but had significant controls in this area. It is noted that the iron is also hot, like the fire of the lights of the previous drawings. It is further significant that the ambivalence of the boy toward the stepmother is depicted by the fact that her legs are obvious, but the control of the X-ing of the ironing board acts as a real barrier, as does father. Even though "Dad" seems to be out of the picture with his back toward it, his name is in the largest letters.

Figure 34

Figure 35, drawn by a 12-year-old boy, is quite typical of the types of drawings seen in this area. The shading of the areas below the waist, the "X" in front of the mother's body, the father with the lawnmower or cutting tool, all are recurrent themes in drawings of boys who have problems in competing with the father for the mother's affection. This K-F-D reiterates the theme of the exacerbation of the Oedipal situation in early adolescence.

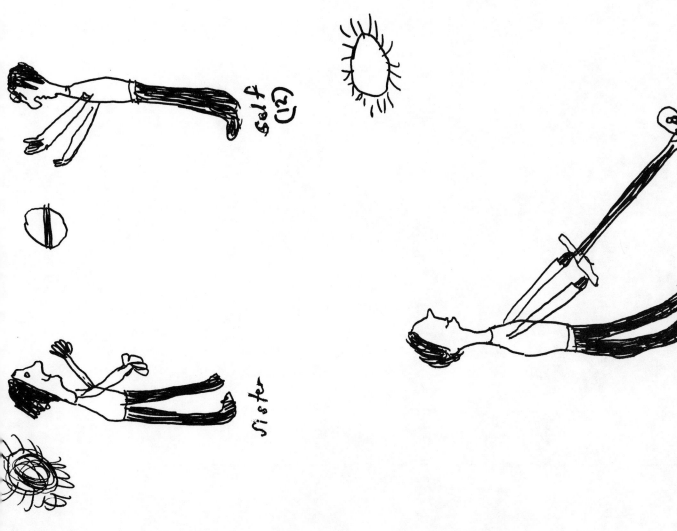

Figure 35

Mother

self
(12)

Sister

Father

In some drawings by clever children, the phenomena may be depicted in other ways. Mark, a 12-year-old boy, who definitely is identifying with the father, draws the theme with the "X" in front of the mother as she carries the lamp. The boy, however, looks a great deal like the father. He is carrying an object quite identical to the father's and we see relatively normal identification attempts as he marches toward manhood. (An uphill effort?)

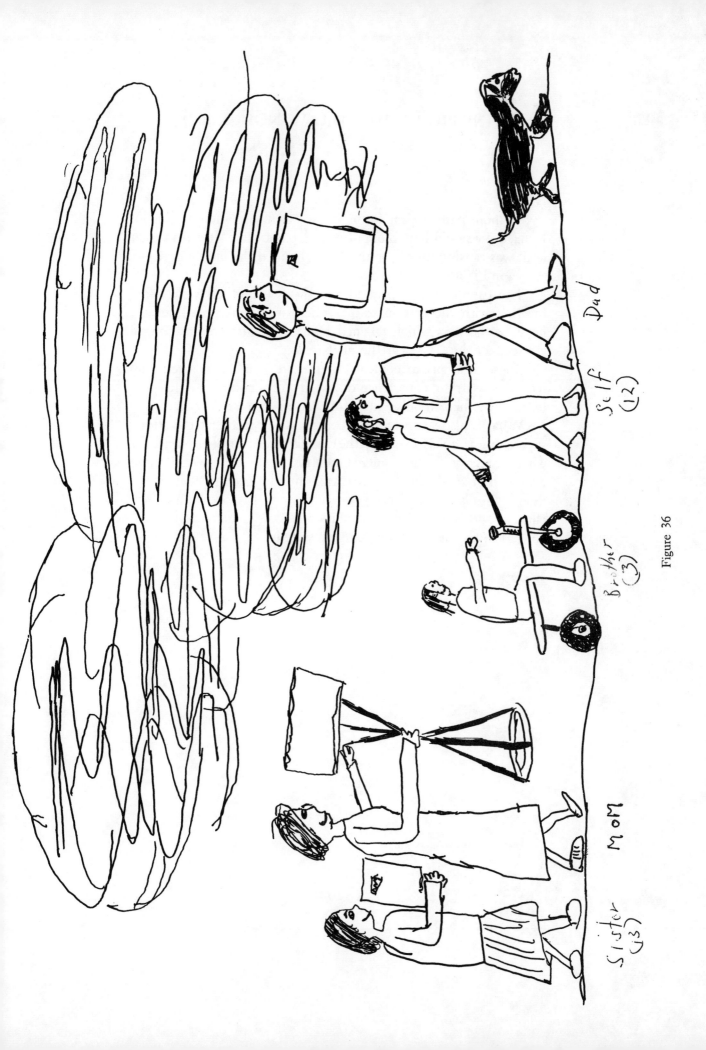

Figure 36

In more pathological forms we see drawings such as that of Dana, a 9-year-old boy, brought in in a panic state. It wasn't clear what was causing this panic until we obtained the family drawing, shown in Figure 37.

The parents were separated and the two brothers were living together with the paternal aunt. There was homosexual activity between the boys which terrified Dana. The attempts at control are seen in the "X" near the anal region.

These attempts to control impulse are seen in children who have a very strong conscience or superego function, and are quite terrified by their impulse and often have severe anxiety states.

What is also significant, of course, is the fact that the strong superego was able to handle the child's needs until such a time when events precipitated increased stress, both from without and from within, as signified by increased impulse activity, so that the usual controls that had been functioning up to then became less efficient and the child needed reinforcement. If not readily available, as in the case of Dana, panic resulted.

Figure 37

# 8

# BOYS' IDENTIFICATION

# WITH POWER

Many boys are able to work out their competitive drives in socially acceptable ways. This is especially true in our culture where most overt competition in the forms of work or sports or academic achievement is acceptable behavior.

For example, 13-year-old Brian's drawing is shown in Figure 38.

He has become very wrapped up in sports and football. The mother often accompanies him to his football games and practice and he tends to capture the mother's time and attention and love through his competitiveness in the football area. While his father is still a threatening figure, the boy draws close to the

Figure 38

mother and gains self-esteem through sublimation of his competitive drives.

It is significant also that father is depicted as a "chopping" man, but is busy doing constructive work around the house. He may make it impossible for the male siblings to compete with him. The brother is sitting calmly on a chair and the patient, himself, is being depicted as an athlete. In order to achieve masculine, accepted behavior, one must revert to sports which father seems disinterested in and which gains mother's approval.


Tom, a 7-year-old boy, tends to sublimate in another very common way for boys. His drawing is shown in Figure 39.

When Tom made his drawing, he started with a small figure of himself and when he reached the waist he paused, scribbled, and this continued furiously. He turned the bottom part of his body into a powerful boat and in this way he is close to the mother and controls her. It is noted in this drawing that the boy insisted on putting the father and the dog on the reverse of the drawing and wants to save the whole front page for himself and his mother.

This boy's Oedipal strivings are sublimated only in the drawing and then in a not very covert way. The shading, the phallic boat, the nude mother and the relegating of the father and the pet to the opposite side is of obvious significance. But here again, the age of the child must be considered if one thinks of a degree of pathology. He is in the midst of his Oedipal strivings.

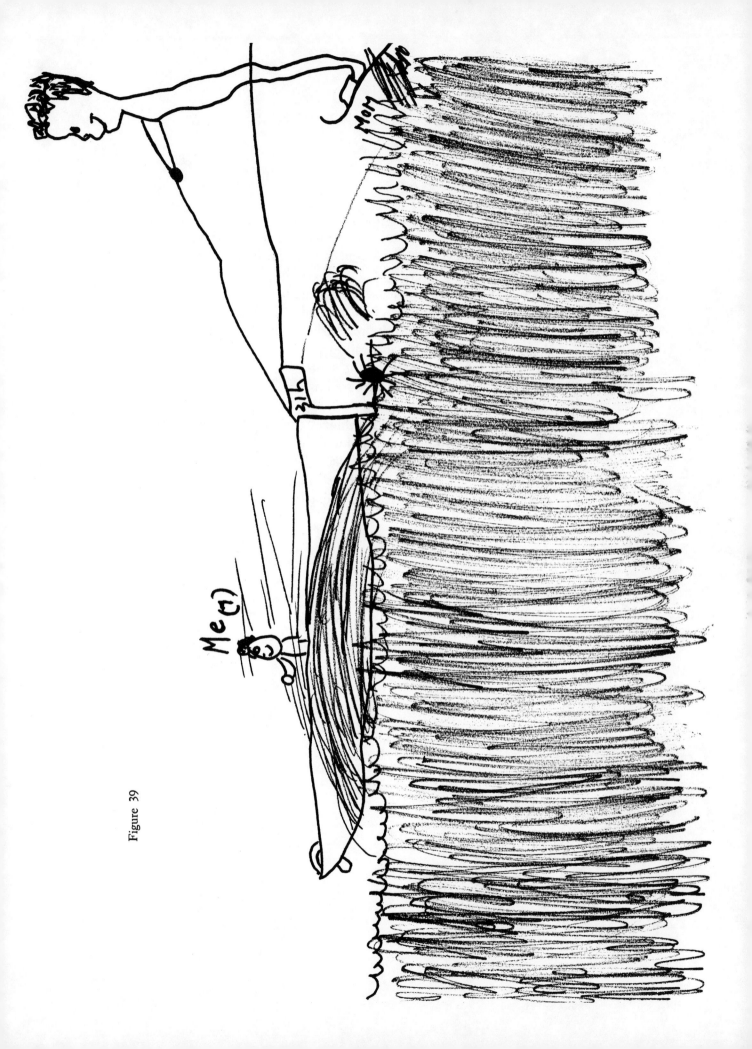

Figure 39

This need for power is pathetically demonstrated in Drawing 40. Gary, a 16-year-old boy, was brought in for recurrent stealing of motor bikes. When asked to make his drawing, he started with the father and brother. The 12-year-old brother is very good in sports and very close to the father because of this. Gary was unable to compete in this area. When he made the drawing of himself, as did Tom in Figure 39, he reached the waist area, paused, and then proceeded with an intricate depiction of himself as part of the motor bike in pursuit of the mother. This boy's compulsive stealing of bikes became a very serious problem for which he was institutionalized.

Again, the boy compartmentalizes the drawing, isolating the father and the brother from him and derives all of his feelings of self-worth and power from the bike. Without the motor bike he felt inadequate as a person. The stealing and the possession of mother seem to be frighteningly equated.

Figure 40

Figure 41 shows the struggle for power and self-worth in 16-year-old John, who makes himself the central figure in the drawing. Again, he identifies with the car and derives a great deal of power from it. It is noted that the car is passing over the father who is depicted as the king in the family, with a crown. The boy is between the father and the mother and close to the mother. We note the repetition of the "X" phenomena below the mother's waist, although this is much more controlled and shows a compulsive way to control anxiety. But the same problems of control and impulse appear, which the boy sublimates through identification with the power of the car.

With the car he can overpower the king, and become the biggest and most powerful in the entire kingdom (family).

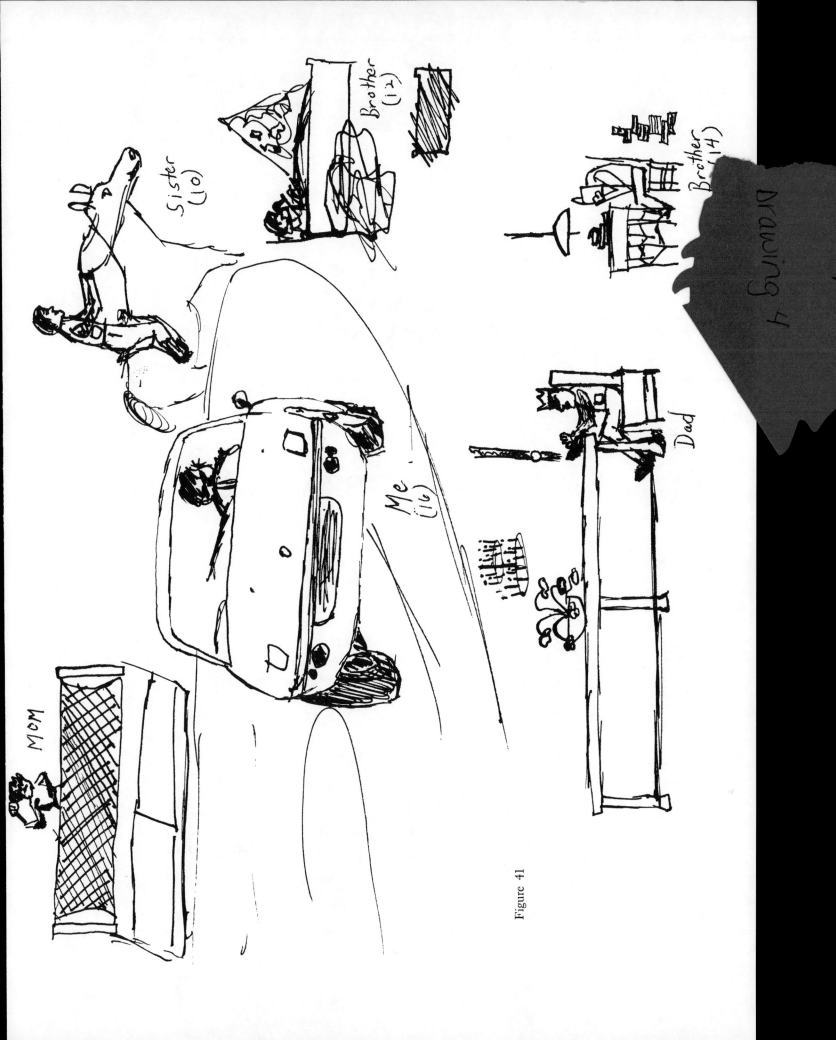

Figure 41

# 9

# GENERAL KINETIC ASPECTS

# OF

# FAMILY DRAWINGS

The activities of the members of the family in the drawing have been discussed in previous drawings. In this chapter we would like to look more carefully at the forces between the figures in the drawings.

For example, 14-year-old Billy, who drew Figure 42, has recently acquired a new stepfather, who brought two stepsisters into the family. Billy was brought in because of behavioral disturbances in the schoolground, as well as acting out at home.

One notes in his drawing the forces between the two families. The boy is attempting to protect the mother from the intruding

Figure 42

step-sister (B)

step Dad

step-sister (A)

Me

Mom

sister (C)

father, and the competitiveness of the males again is shown clearly in the forces in the picture.

The patient must be aware of the sexual relationship between the stepfather and the mother, as the sword between the stepfather's legs is the largest weapon in the drawing. The boy shooting his small darts cannot hurt the father, who protects himself with the shield while the boy's darts break harmlessly. So the boy, recognizing the sexuality of the relationship, also at the same time recognizes his impotency, which might very well account for his angry acting-out behavior.

Jim, a 10-year-old boy whose drawing is shown in Figure 43, shows a more normal force between himself and the father. In the drawing it is depicted as an airplane. This, again, is a boy who has a new foster mother. He is attempting to get close to her and has competition with the father for the new mother's affection. Note the glaring light above the picture, which again is a common theme in the boy's struggle for love and affection.

Here, in contrast to the destructive struggle seen between fathers and sons in some of the drawings, where dangerous or hurting implements are thrown at each other, in this drawing where the boy is striving for acceptance the "weapon" is a paper airplane.

MOTHER MAKING DINNER

JIM
Me(o)

DAD THROWING BACK + FORTH PLANE TO JIM

JEFF

Figure 43

Figure 44 again shows the forces within the drawing. Ron, the 10-year-old boy, has a father who has a "bad back" and is extremely irritable. The boy has difficulty identifying with him and struggles to get some affection from the mother. Note the force coming from the brother's mouth to blow the father down and the counterforce from the father with the hammer descending. Ron is a very clever boy and as he moves toward the father, he does this high above him and swings down to the tree to where the mother is planting and where the boy can receive some love and affection from the mother.

It is significant also to mention that it is not only difficult to identify with a sick or injured father, but the usual free flow of anger which the strong and healthy father can withstand or block off is interfered with, and the ill or castrated father becomes an inhibitor to the child's normal aggression. It may make the child wish for omnipotence so that he can actually destroy the weakened father, but this his super-ego cannot allow.

Figure 44

The force between sibs is often depicted as a ball.

Figure 45 shows a very primitive drawing by a 6-year-old. He has great rivalry with his 10-year-old sister.

This 6-year-old apparently is still struggling within the Oedipal situation, struggling for identification, and one can surmise that the shading of everyone's genital area and using a ball as the instrument of force may very well depict the child's sexual preoccupations.

Figure 45

In Figure 46 we see an 11-year-old boy, who is extremely competitive with the father. He tends to try to act out this competitiveness.

The force between him and his father again is of a healthy type, but this is the drawing of a very competitive boy. There is another interesting part of this drawing—the fact that he crossed out his first picture of himself, which depicted a very aggressive face, and turned himself around so one could see only the violent throwing of the ball, which is acceptable. But the violence of his face is turned away.

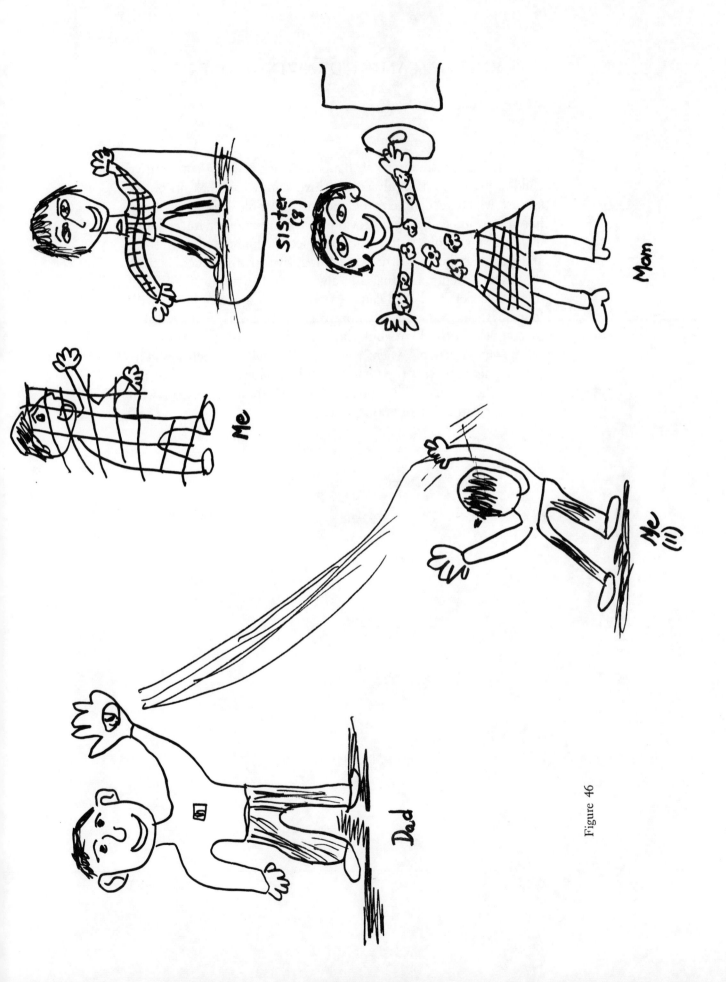

Figure 46

Drawing 47 shows what happens when a very competitive child is placed in a highly competitive family, but has no object against which to compete. Diana, an 8-year-old girl, was placed in a foster home. She had previously lived in another foster home with her 7-year-old sister. She completely dominated this sister and was described as extremely competitive. In the school setting the teacher mentioned that she always wanted responsibility and to be a leader in class. Diana was placed in a foster home with four boys, the youngest of whom was 13. She very much wanted to compete with them, but did not know how, and thus was acting out in school, where she was extremely competitive. The drawing again reflects the force of the ball. However, it is directed toward the ground. The girl has not yet found a person with whom she can compete in this family.

Figure 47

Figure 48, drawn by a 14-year-old boy, depicts another problem in the sibling rivalry, or forces between sibs. Mike has a brother, age 13, who is mentally retarded. It is noted that there is no force between the boys, but rather the ball or the force is all invested in the retarded brother. It is, of course, difficult to compete with someone who is handicapped as it induces guilt feelings. While the boy does have competitive feelings with the brother for the father's affection, he is unable to have active competition with him and tends to sublimate this through the painting he is doing in the drawing.

Even though this family is not compartmentalized, the outstanding theme seems to be poor communication. No one faces another. People have their sides or their backs to each other and each is preoccupied with his "own thing."

Mom

Dad

Brother
(13)

Sister

Me
(14)

Figure 48

Karen is a 7-year-old girl, who was seen because the family is in a state of divorce. The anxiety that she has is shown by the scribbling between the two parents, which is an almost literal translation of the stress and strain of the divorce procedure and the little girl's reaction to this as seen in Figure 49.

This drawing seems depressive; even the sun is blacked out, but one would think that the youngest in the family, "Mike," seems to be the only one rising above everything, with his kite.

Figure 49

SISTER

me

BROTHER
(5)

BROTHER

dad

mom

Tommy, a 10-year-old boy, produced the family action shown in Figure 50.

The boy has a very busy father who is away from home a great deal in his work as a surgeon. The boy has a very domineering mother who always wants him to achieve. She makes him practice the piano, but even when the mother is in various parts of the house, as soon as Tommy hits the wrong note she has to come and watch him. Thus, by failing on the piano he attempts to control and show passive-aggressiveness towards the mother. Note the distance of the father in the drawing and the intervening wall between the boy and the father. The drawing also reflects difficulties in the learning situation and the secondary gain in controlling the parents' attention by not achieving.

One wonders if the sister escapes by being so high and "out of it."

School achievement is, of course, a central factor in many families and is reflected in many of the family drawings, as shown in the next chapter.

Figure 50

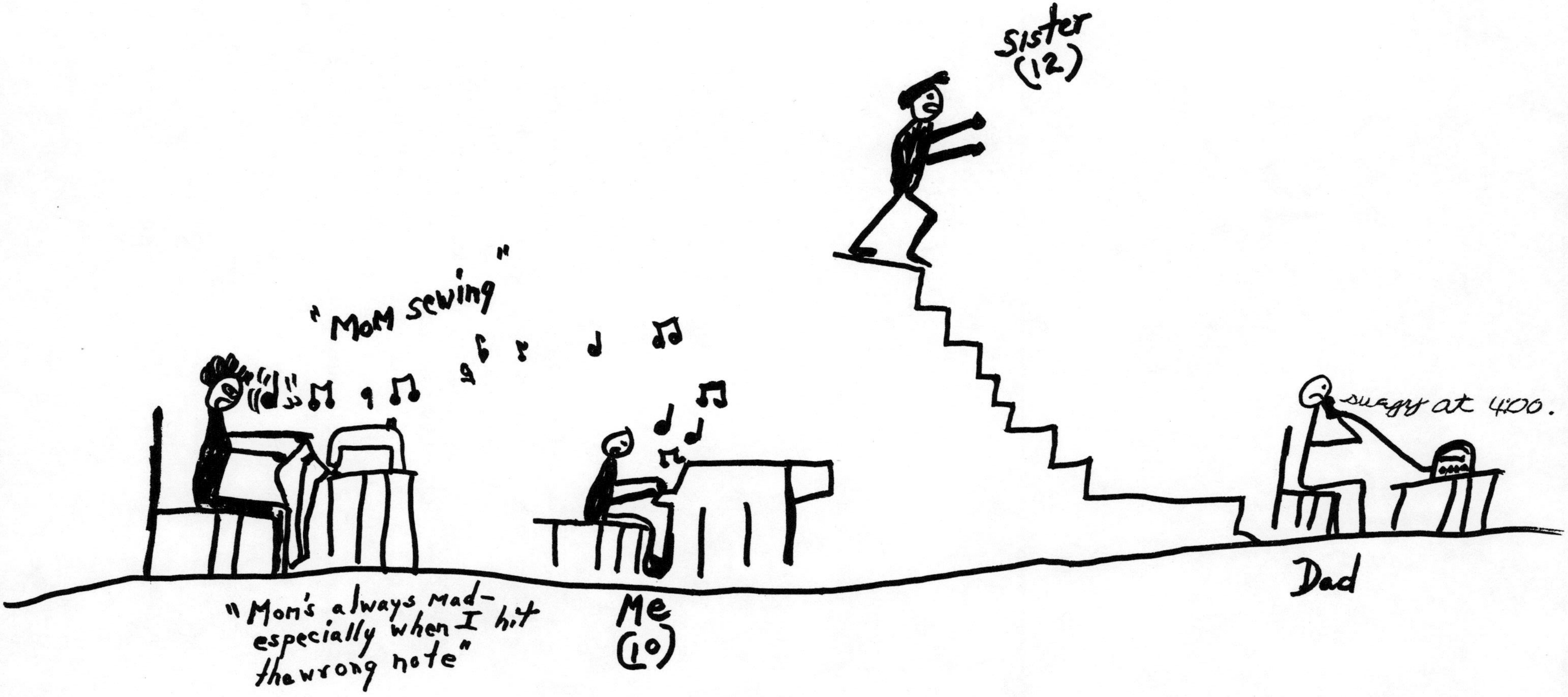

# 10

# SCHOOL

# PROBLEMS

*The "A" Syndrome:*

The "A" syndrome was first recognized rather dramatically through the K-F-D of a 16-year-old girl brought in with unusual symptoms. She had worked in the principal's office for the past two years and had obtained a number of report cards which she had falsified to depict herself as almost a straight "A" student, when indeed she was a "C−" student. In Nancy's drawing, shown in Figure 51, note the scribbling below the mother's waist. In this case, this is anxiety because the mother had had surgery several times and the girl did not identify with the mother, who was thought to have cancer. Rather, she tended to identify with the

134

Figure 51

youngest child in the family, Jack, age 7. When Nancy's K-F-D was first reviewed, the "A's," which were the posts for the swing, were not noticed. But they became extremely obvious when one understood the girl's presenting problems, and her desire to be young again and to get the love and affection that one often receives from parents through very high school achievement. However, because of her concerns and regressive tendencies, she was unable to achieve, but did so through her forgery.

Figure 52, drawn by 9-year-old Mike, perhaps more clearly demonstrates the "A syndrome."

The father in this case was the principal of a school and put a great deal of pressure on the boy to do his homework and to achieve at a very high level. Note the "A" which is the dominant force between the father and the son, and again the cutting attitude of the father and the precarious position of the boy in relation to the father and the "A."

It also seemed significant that the patient is caught between the mother and father, while the two teen-age brothers have gotten out in a car or in a band. The 9-year-old still needs mother's cooking and balances precariously in his relationship to father on an "A," even though father threatens this balance.

Figure 52

Figure 53 was produced by a 9-year-old girl, who was a twin. She and her sister were highly competitive and had not established a dominant-submissive pattern, as most twins do. Each girl was very jealous of the other girl in school and if one obtained an "A," the other was heartbroken. The swinging of the two girls between "A's" (depicted by the supports of the swing) was clearly seen. "A's" dominate the world of this family.

Figure 53

*School Phobias and School Refusals:*

Oftentimes children are unable to achieve in school because of their worry and concern for other members of the family. Very frequently we see children who refuse to go to school and very high in frequency is some concern about a member of the family. Drawing 54, by Paul, an 8-year-old boy, simply and clearly depicts the concerns in children who do have a school phobia.

The mother had recently had surgery. In the drawing, the boy is very close to her and it is obvious that she is the closest thing to him and his concern for her well-being is apparent.

This is of special significance because many so-called "school phobias" are actually "school refusals." The latter phrase seems preferable because it isn't that the child is afraid of school, but that the child's concern is primarily with what is going to happen at home when she or he is not there. The child is primarily concerned that his own unacceptable wishes may very well be recognized and may actually be acted out and the parent destroyed or hurt in some way.

Figure 54

In more chronic and severe forms of school phobias, we see the drawing such as that in Figure 55 by Brad, a 10-year-old boy.

The mother was quite depressed and chronically in bed and ill. The older brother was a severely retarded boy. The father had fairly well left the family. He came home only to eat and sleep, but did not interact with other members of the family. The separation of the family group in the drawing is interesting, with the father isolated in one corner. The boy attempts to identify with the older sister, but the shading and the drawing of the mother and the older brother and their prone positions suggest the boy's concern about the possibility of their death. This boy has missed a great deal of school, often has somatic complaints and will do many things to stay home and make sure the family is still alive.

In this instance, one can hypothesize with some degree of accuracy the fact that the relationship with the mother and probably with the older brother is one of frightening hostility. Brad must have very disturbing, destructive thoughts toward each of them; the brother, for obvious reasons, and the mother because she is always ill and therefore abandoning her motherly duties and, in turn, causing the boy to also lose his father by her behavior. These hostile feelings are so strong that the child must remain at home to protect himself from acting out his hostility.

Figure 55

Figure 56 shows the drawing of a little 8-year-old girl who has a father who is very ill. The girl spends a great deal of time playing with animals and she refuses to go to school.

This little girl may have to protect her sick father from the mother. This may very well be part of her phantasies in the midst of her Oedipal problems. It would be impossible for her to go to school and leave her father unprotected.

Figure 56

Dad
"He's sick"

MOM
"Drawing a chart
for church"

picking up
paper
Me
(8)

drinking from
a faucet

Brother
(5)

Figure 57 was drawn by 9-year-old Carol. It shows significant regressive tendencies and attempts to compete with the younger sibs. This girl tends to become quite depressed. It is noted in the drawing that she has isolated herself under a table with food on top, and the 3-year-old brother is encapsulated in this small area with her. Note again the "X" phenomena. She has anger directed toward the younger sib, but finds this unacceptable and tends to direct her anger inward. The rest of the family is depicted on the water fishing and is quite distant from the world of herself and the 3-year-old. This water theme in drawings is very frequent and associated with significant depressive tendencies.

Figure 57

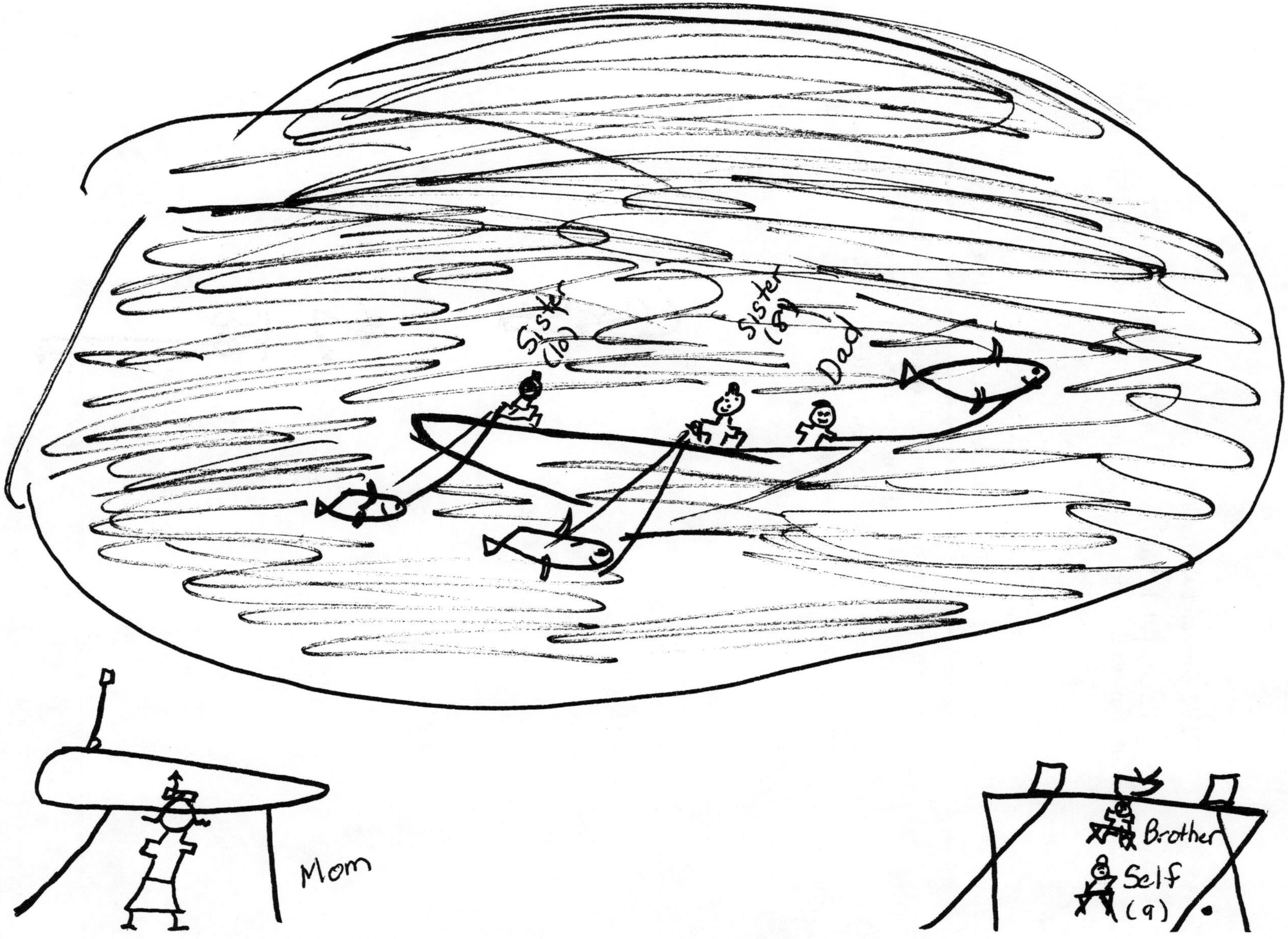

*Depressions and Water Themes*

Preoccupation with water is a recurrent theme in K-F-D's as it is in many projective tests such as the Rorschach Inkblot. It is more than a chance factor that many suicides leap into water.

Figure 58 was drawn by Jerry, a 10-year-old boy, who was relatively normal, but whose father had recurrent severe depressive episodes.

Jerry is concerned about father's depression, as the water under the father suggests, but the boy is the only angry looking one in the picture and one wonders how he feels about the casual non-caring hula-dancing mother.

Figure 58

Tony a 9½-year-old boy, produced Figure 59.

The boy became quite despondent when thinking of his father, who actually was in prison at the time the drawing was made. Notice the compartmentalization of the family from the father, with the underwater scene, which is again very common in children with depressive thoughts. In this case the father and his situation seem to be related to the primary dynamics of the boy's hostility and depression.

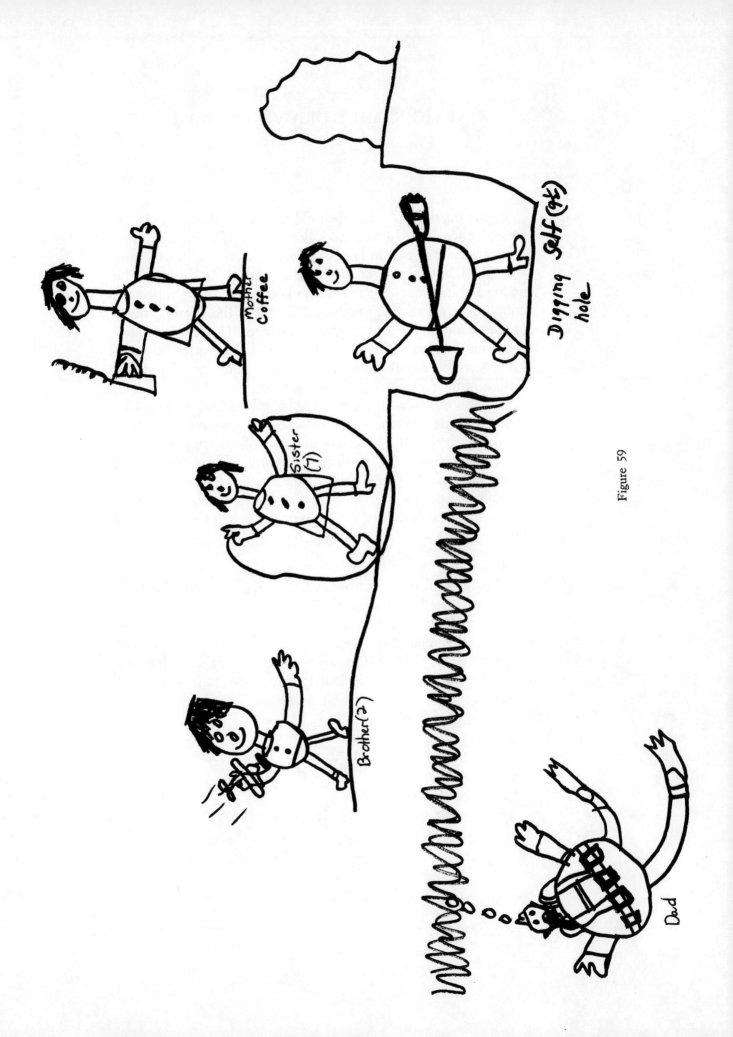

Figure 59

Figure 60, drawn by a 10-year-old boy, again shows significant depressive reaction. In this case, the mother is doing the usual things that mothers do in family drawings. That is, she is cooking or doing other things to take care of the family. In this case, the mother has had four surgeries in the last ten months. Notice the scribbling on the mother's body and the tilt of the drawing, showing the distortions of his thoughts in this area. He depicts himself as floating in a rather helpless way in a pool of water and again this reflects his actual mood, which was a significant depression because of his mother's health problem.

It makes one think of the horrible birthday scene in the movie, "The Graduate," when, in his new skin diving outfit, the hero walks into and lies at the bottom of the pool, allowing himself to be the pawn of his father's infantile strivings, and yet one has the feeling that only if he could stay at the bottom of the pool could he really escape. Depression, water, returning to the swimming state of prenatal existence, all are brought out in this significant drawing of a 10-year-old depressed boy.

The depression associated with the K-F-D water theme is usually associated with a reaction to specific events, such as an ill parent, a father in prison, a depressed parent, etc. A more generalized and chronic depression is associated with the snow theme, (opposite to the light or heat syndrome), in the K-F-D, but that is another topic and unfortunately our book must end somewhere.

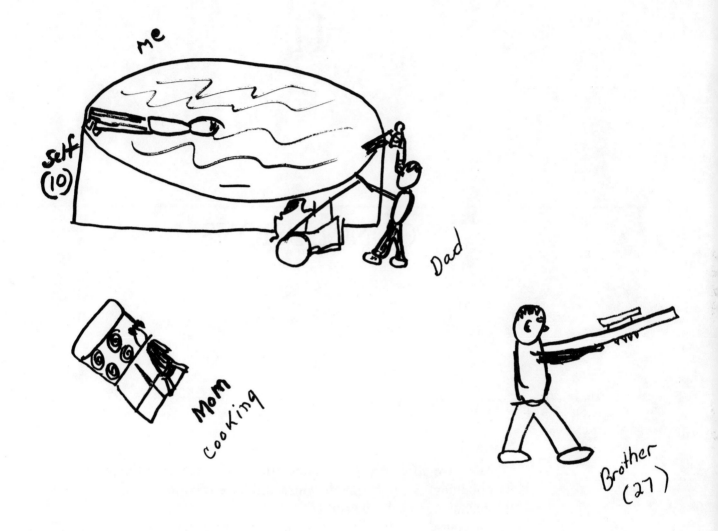

Figure 60

# 11

# CONCLUSIONS

We have attempted to introduce the reader to the technique for obtaining kinetic family drawings and have tried to show how the technique can be meaningful.

Of course, the K-F-D's tell us more than we can understand and we are certain numerous themes such as the "A," "ironing board" and "light" syndromes are waiting to be deciphered. While sixty drawings have been presented as representative of our thousands of drawings, much has by necessity been left unsaid. Chapters were prepared on the "cat" syndrome, "plant" syndrome, "snow" syndrome and others. Because of the richness of the K-F-D's in providing "dynamic" information, we decided to limit our presentation to an introduction of the K-F-D, hoping that some of the excitement we feel in working with this technique can be communicated to the reader. Our own understanding of troubled children has improved since adding movement to their originally inert drawings.

> "Since it is *understanding* that sets man above the rest of sensible beings, and gives him all the advantages and dominion which he has over them, it is certainly a subject worth our labor to inquire into." —*John Locke* (1690)

> Understanding (NOUS)—"Giving *movement,* unity and system to what had previously been a jumble of inert elements."—*Anaxagoras of Clazomenae* (500-428 B.C.)

# REFERENCES

1. BUCK, J. N.: The H-T-P Technique: A Qualitative and Quantitative Scoring Manual. *J. Clin. Psychol.* 4:317-396. 1948
2. BURNS, R. C.: Movement: Key to Understanding Intelligence of the Special Child in Century 21. In Jerome Hellmuth (Ed.), The Special Child in Century 21. *Special Child Publications*. Seattle. 1964.
3. CARPENTER, CLARENCE R.: Naturalistic Behavior of Nonhuman Primates. University Park, Pennsylvania State University Press. 1964.
4. DI LEO, J. H.: Young Children and Their Drawings. Brunner/Mazel. New York. 1970.
5. GOODENOUGH, F. L.: Measurement of Intelligence by Drawings. Harcourt, Brace and World, Inc. New York. 1926.
6. GOODENOUGH, F. L. and HARRIS, D. B.: Studies in the Psychology of Children's Drawings, II: 1928-1949. *Psychol. Bull.* 47:396-433. 1950.
7. HULSE, W. C.: The Emotionally Disturbed Child Draws His Family. *Quart. J. Child Behav.* 3:152-174. 1951.
8. HULSE, W. C.: Childhood Conflict Expressed Through Family Drawings. *J. Proj. Tech.* 16:66-79. 1952.
9. KELLOGG, R.: Analyzing Children's Art. National Press Books. Palo Alto, Calif. 1969.
10. KOPPITZ, E. M.: Psychological Evaluation of Children's Human Figure Drawings. Grune and Stratton, Inc. New York. 1968.
11. MACHOVER, K.: Personality Projection in the Drawing of the Human Figure. Charles C Thomas. Springfield, Ill. 1949.
12. MACHOVER, K.: Human Figure Drawings of Children. *J. Proj. Tech.* 17:85-91. 1953.
13. MACHOVER, K.: Sex Differences in the Developmental Pattern of Children as Seen in Human Figure Drawings. In Rabin and Haworth: Projective Techniques with Children. Grune and Stratton. New York, N. Y. 1960.
14. REZNIKOFF, N. A. and REZNIKOFF, H. R.: The Family Drawing Test: A Comparative Study of Children's Drawings. *J. Clin. Psychol.* 12:167-169. 1956.
15. SCOON, R.: Greek Philosophy Before Plato. Princeton University Press. Princeton. 95-100. 1928.

# INDEX